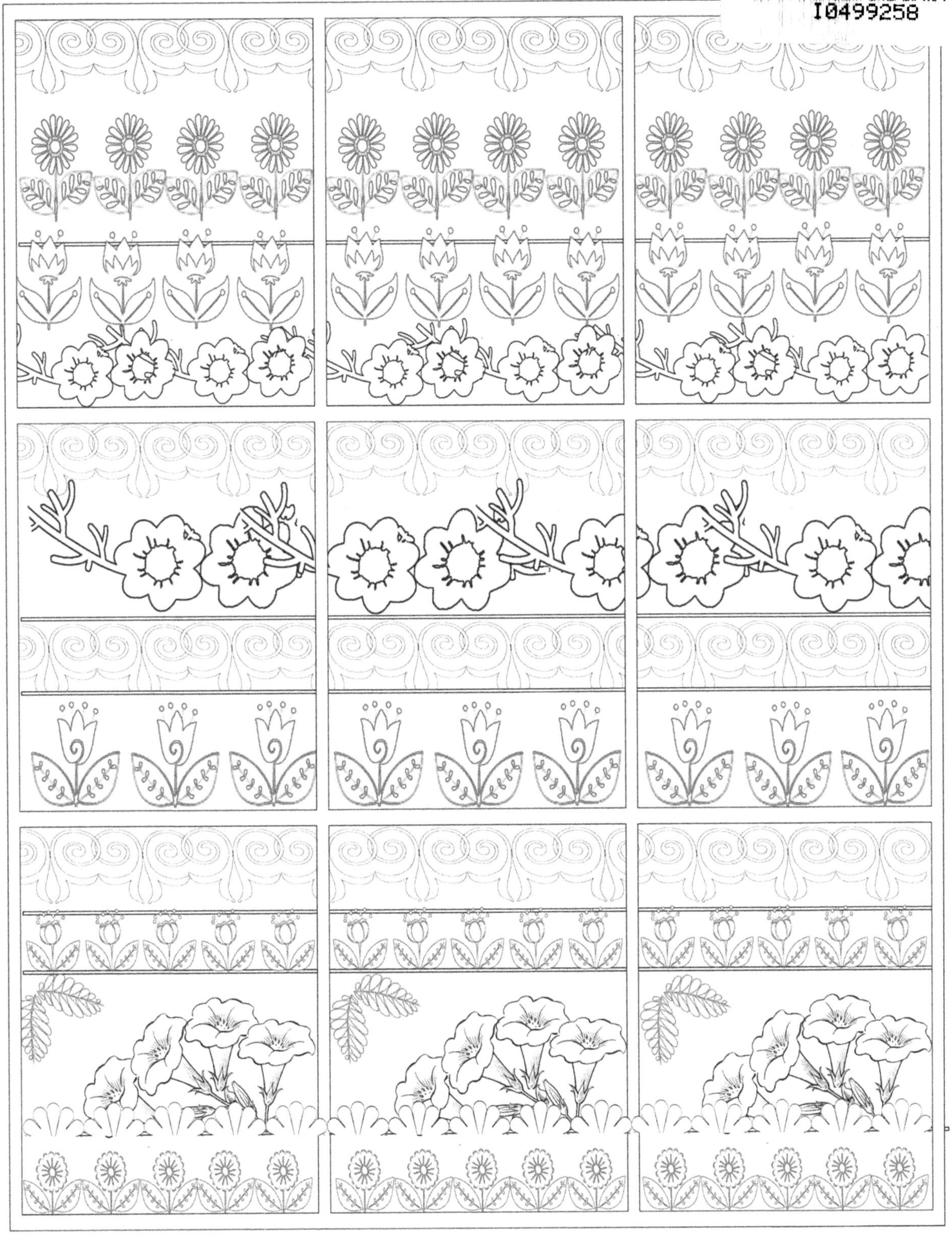

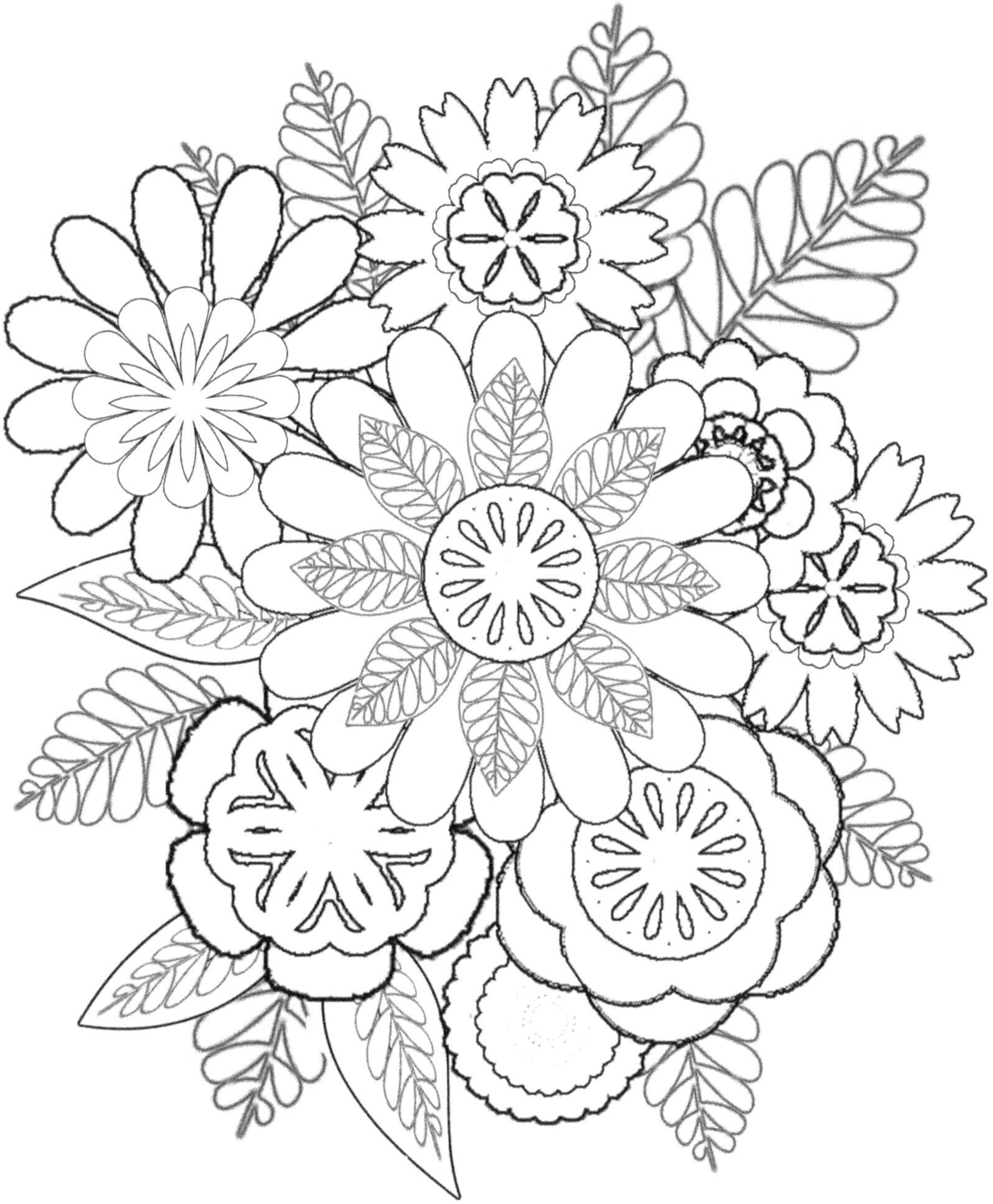

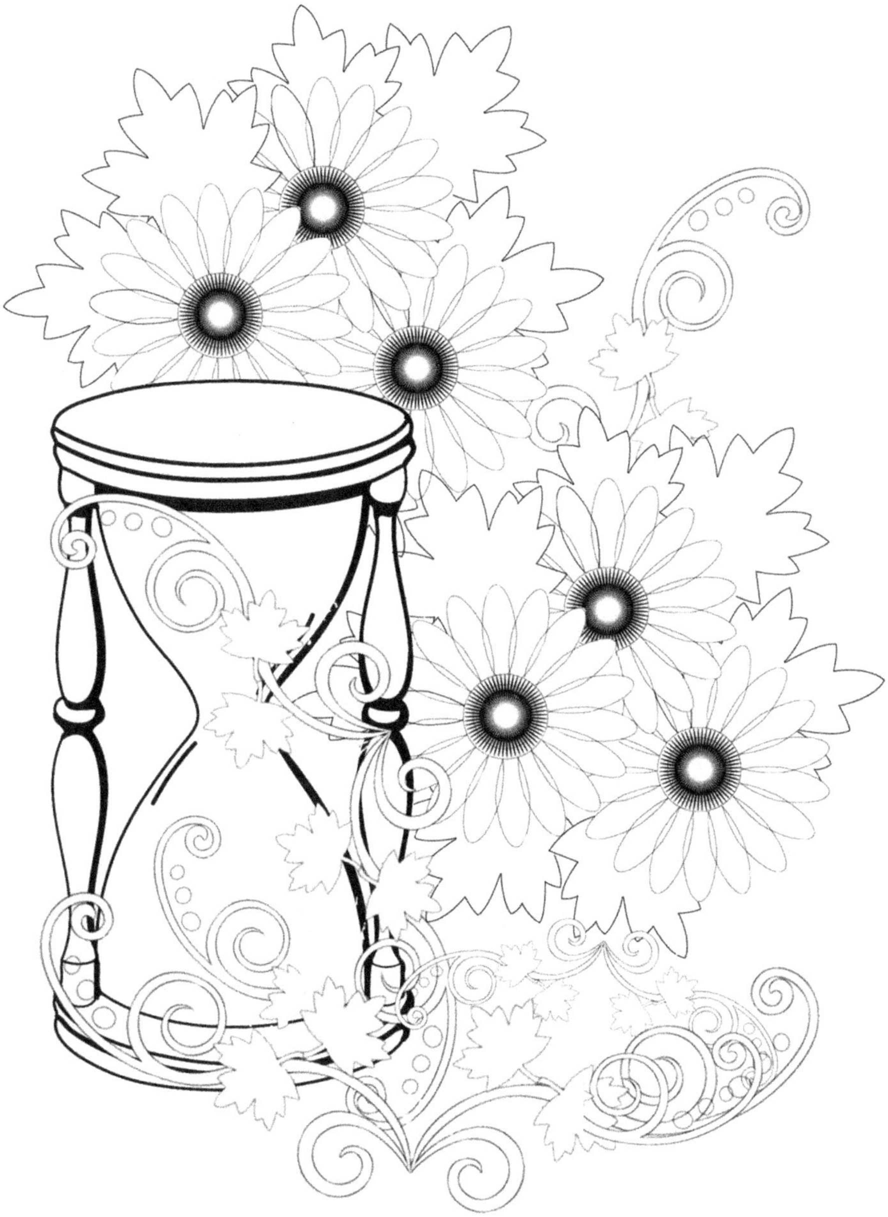

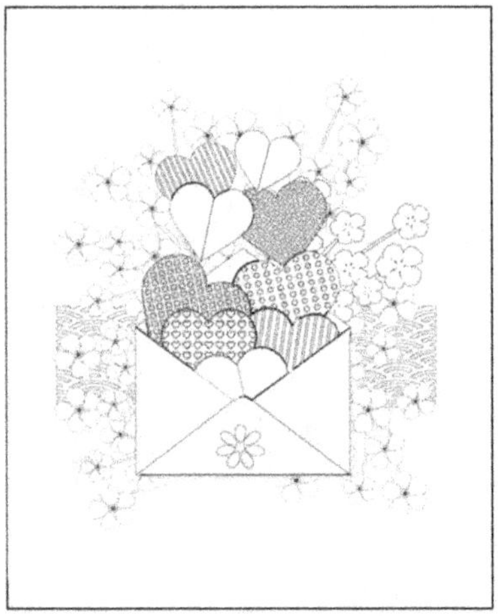
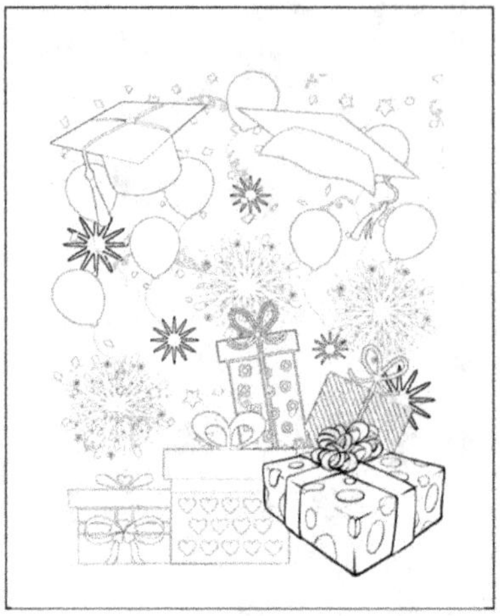
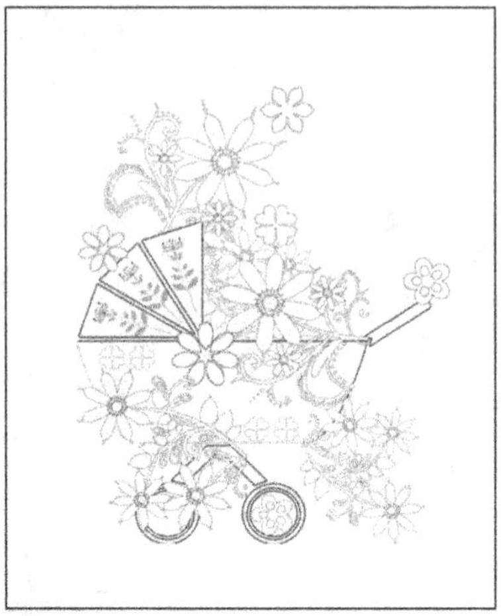
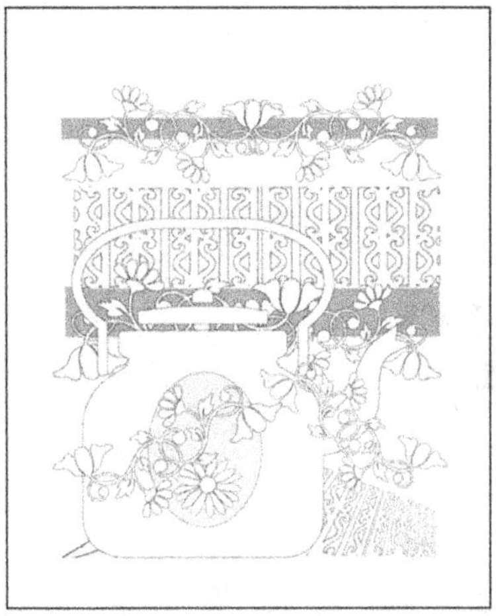
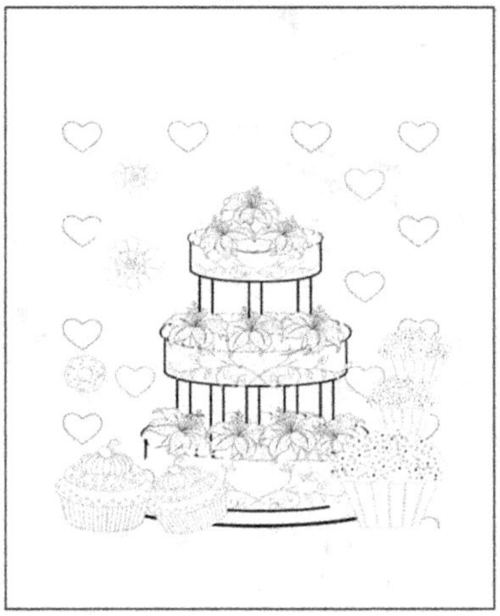
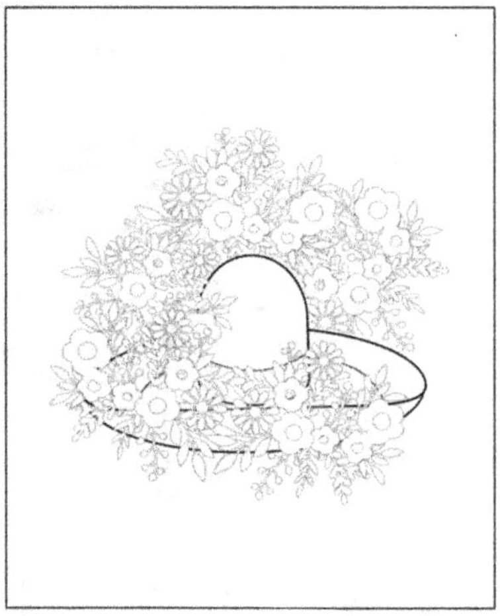
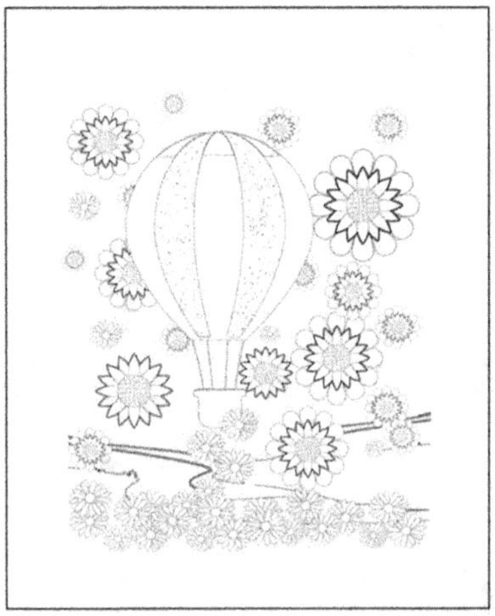
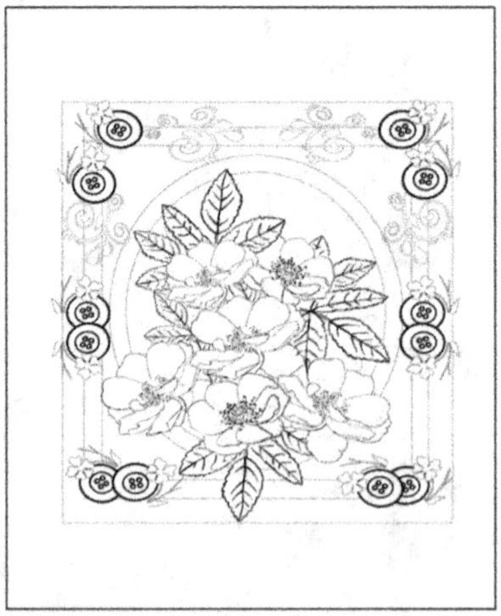
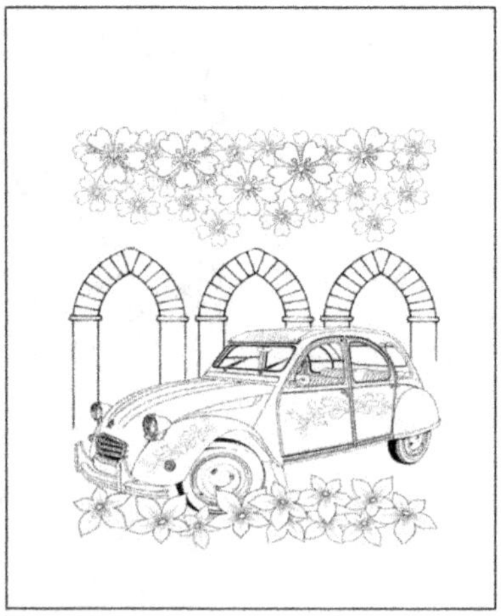

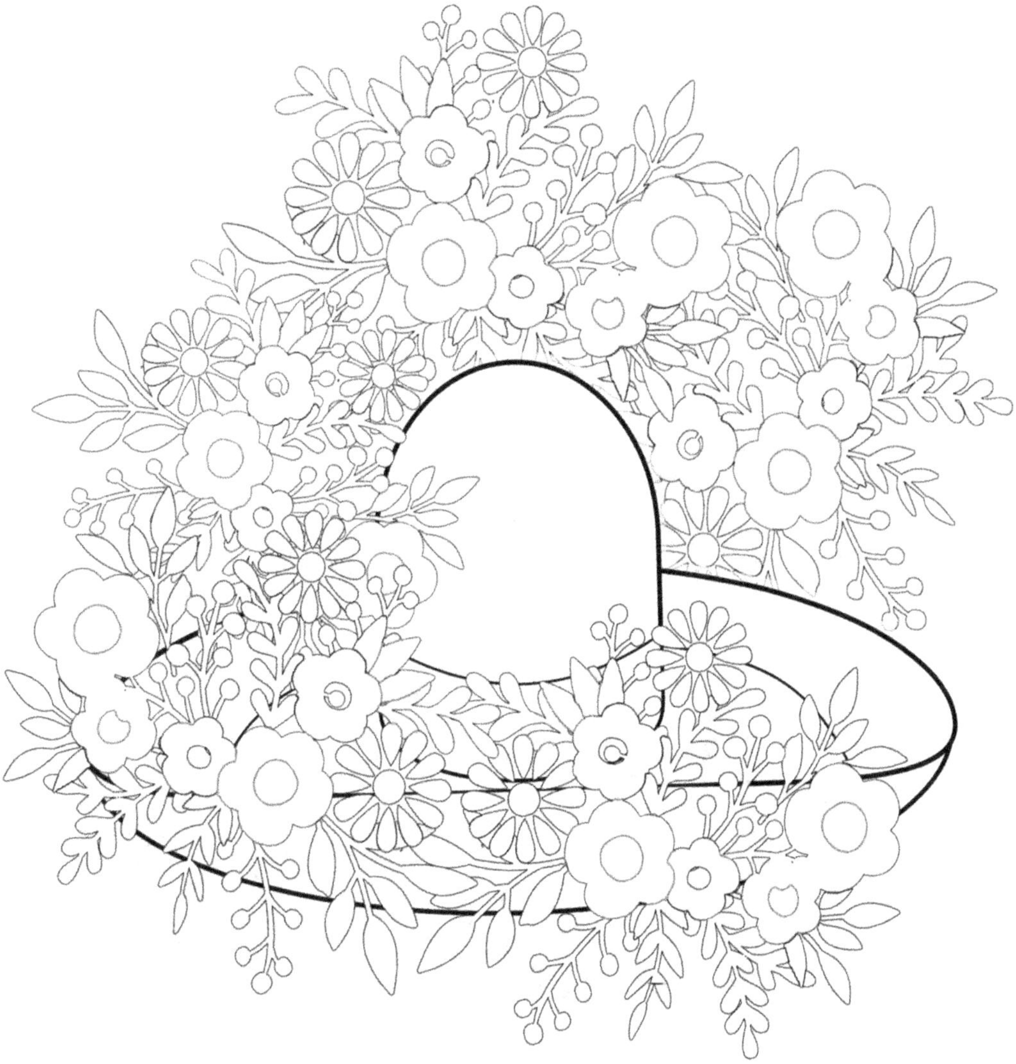

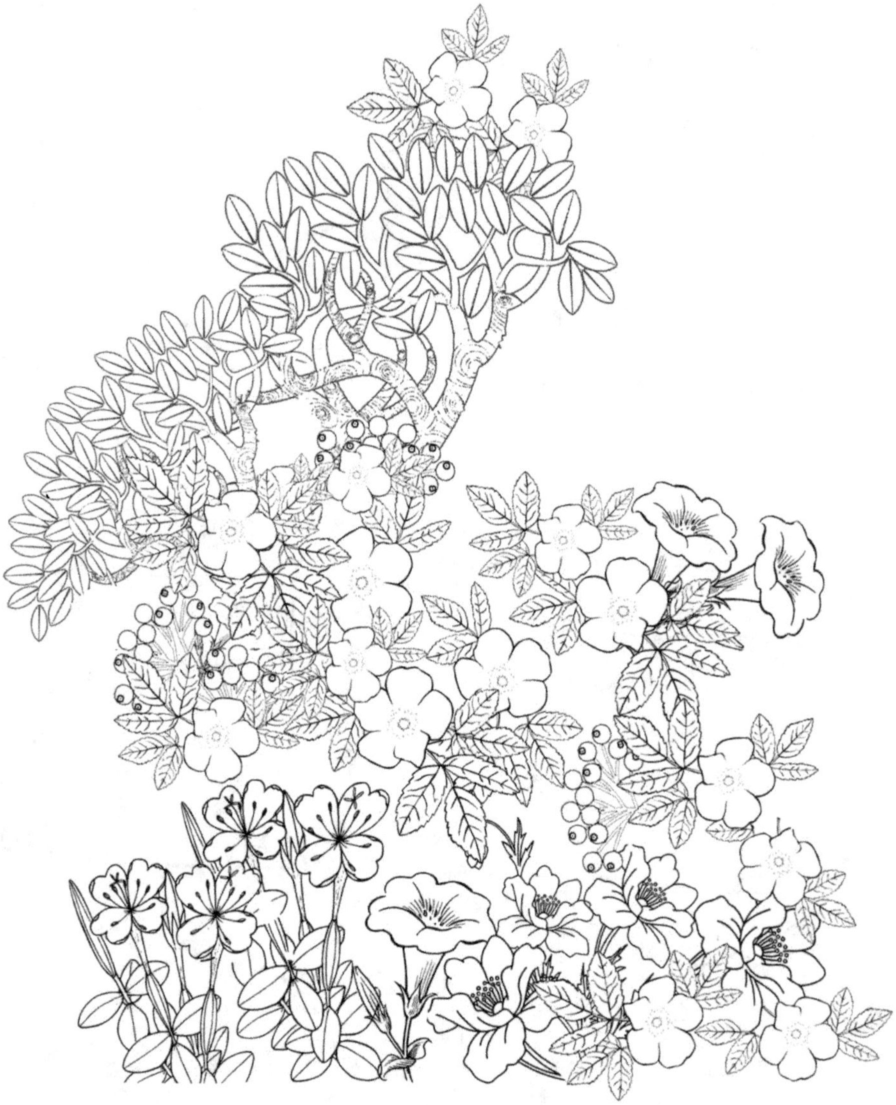

thank you for png tree .com pixabay .com

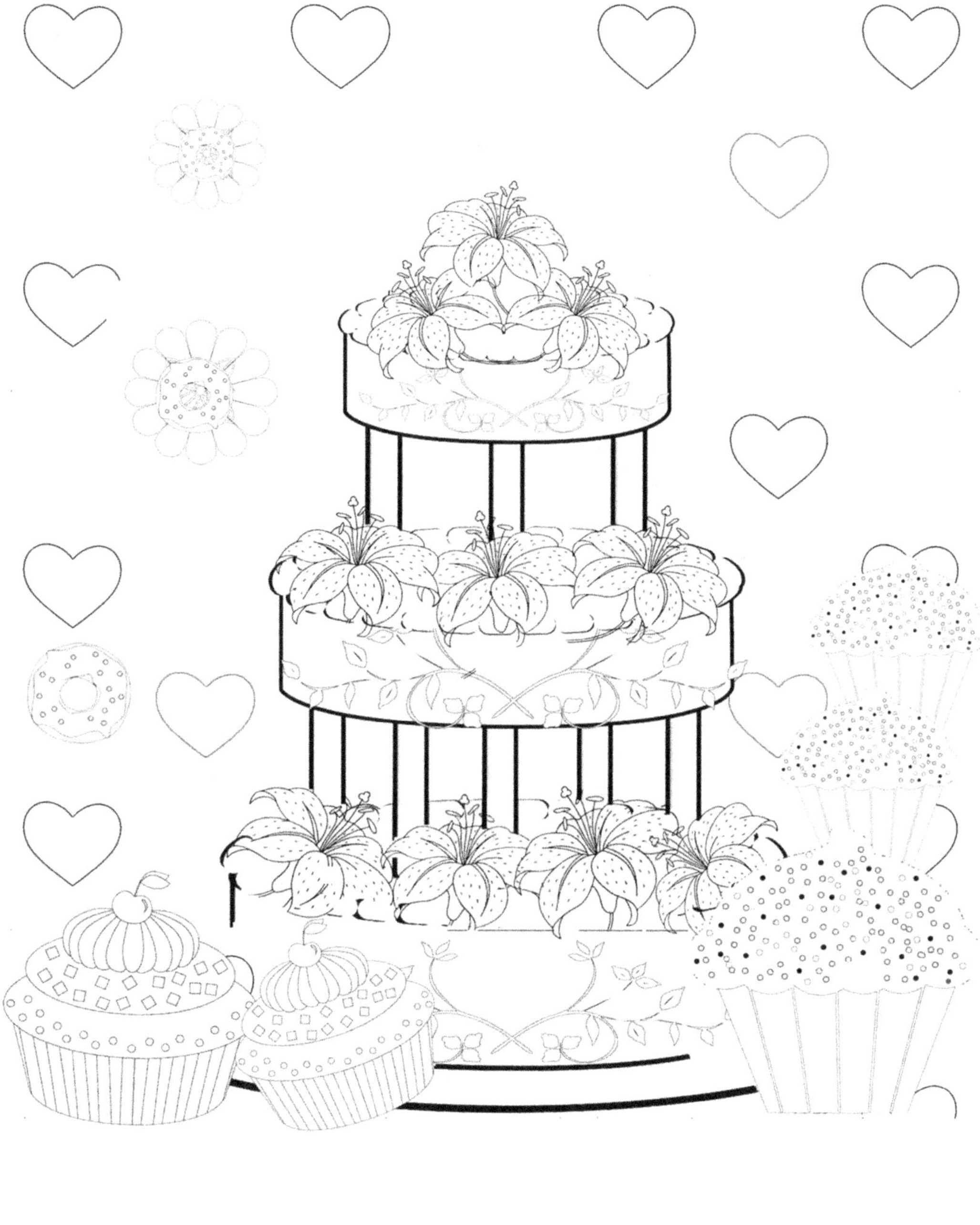

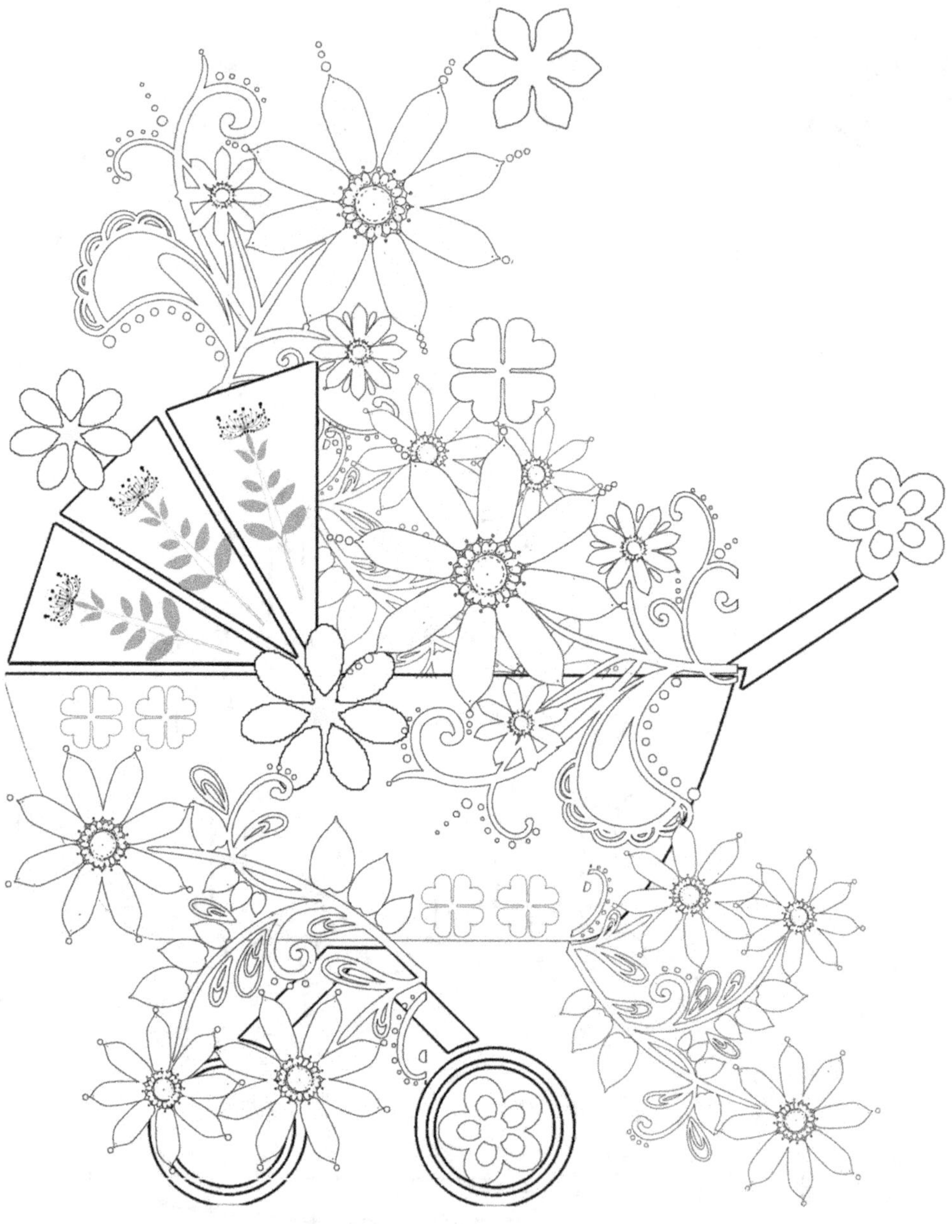

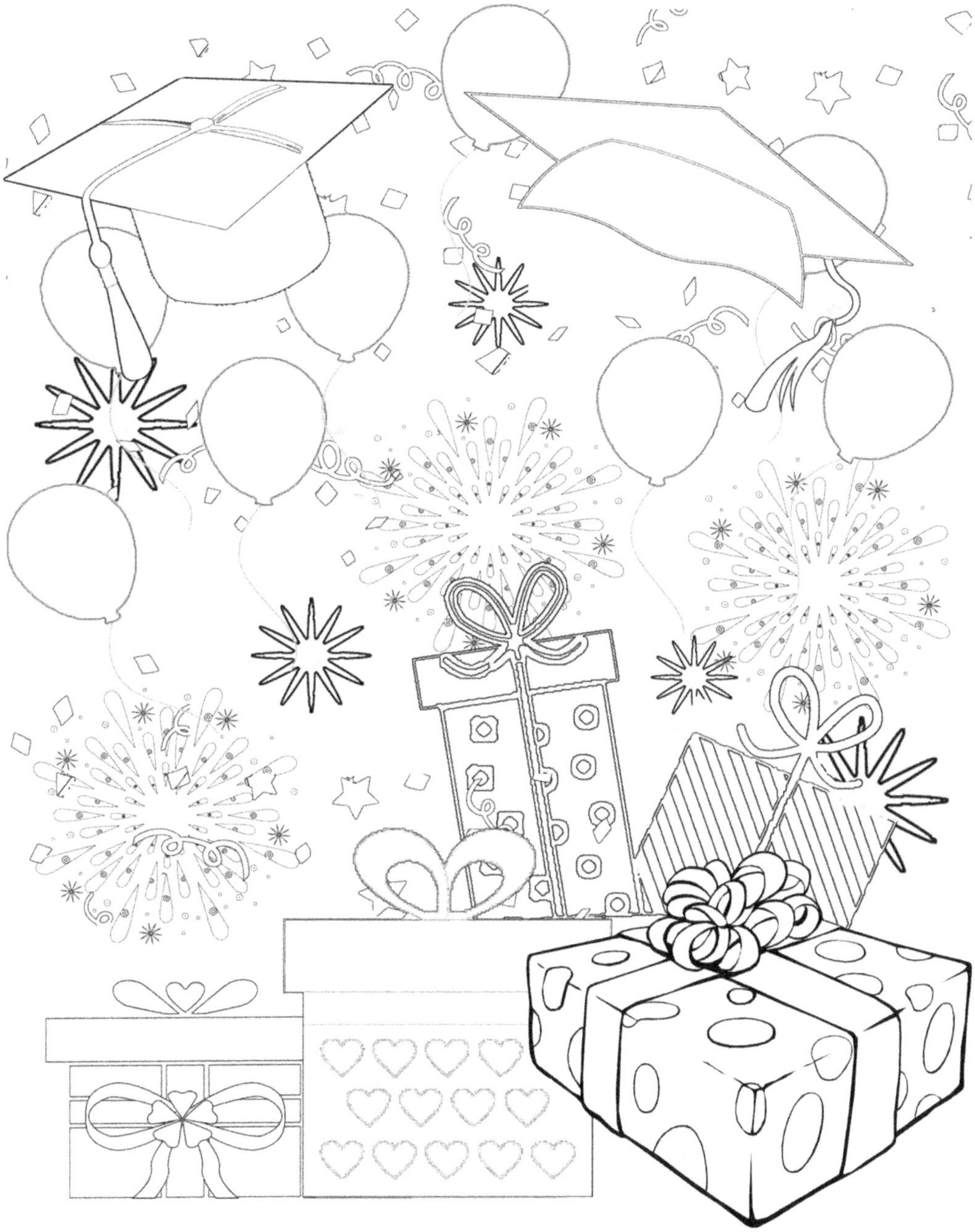

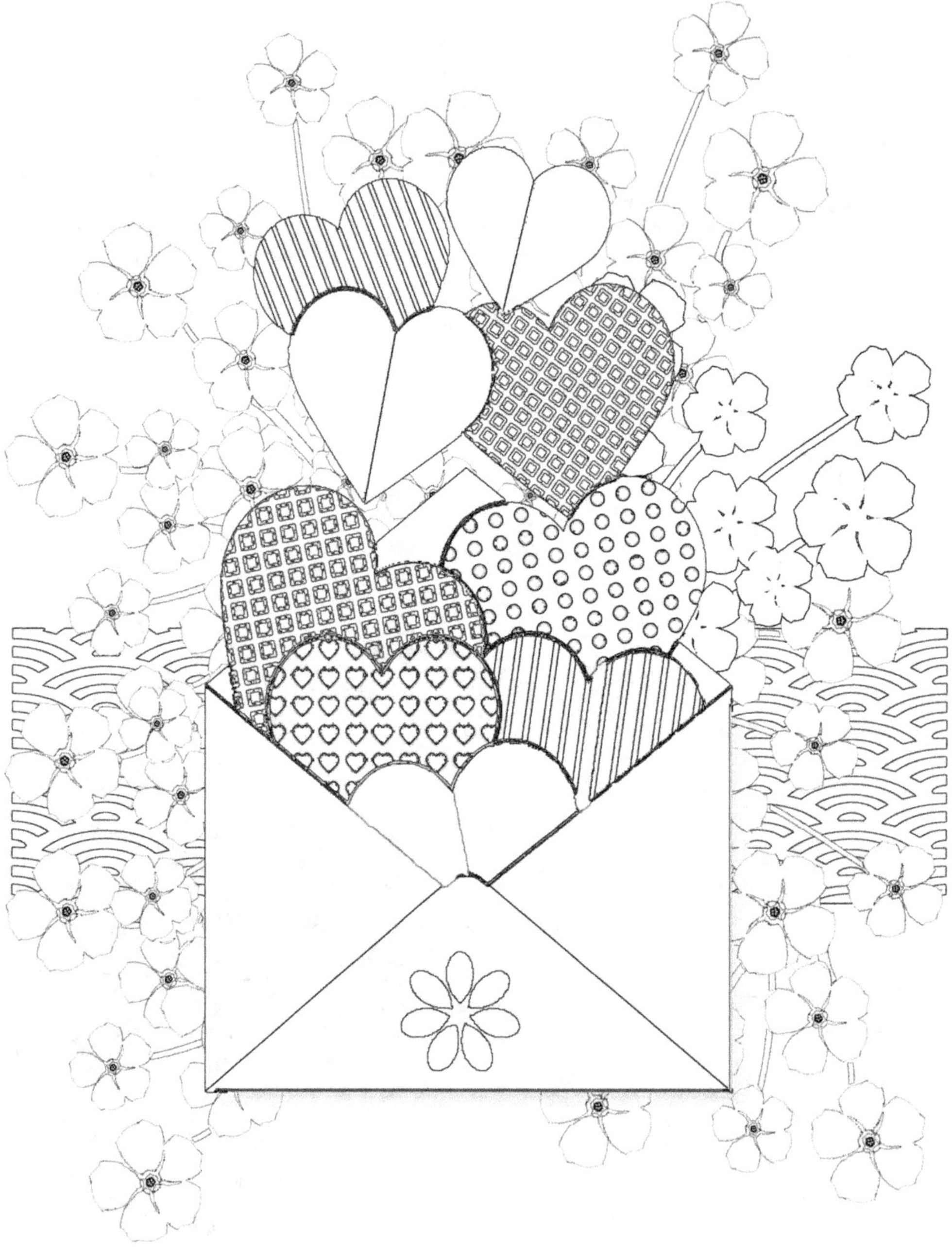

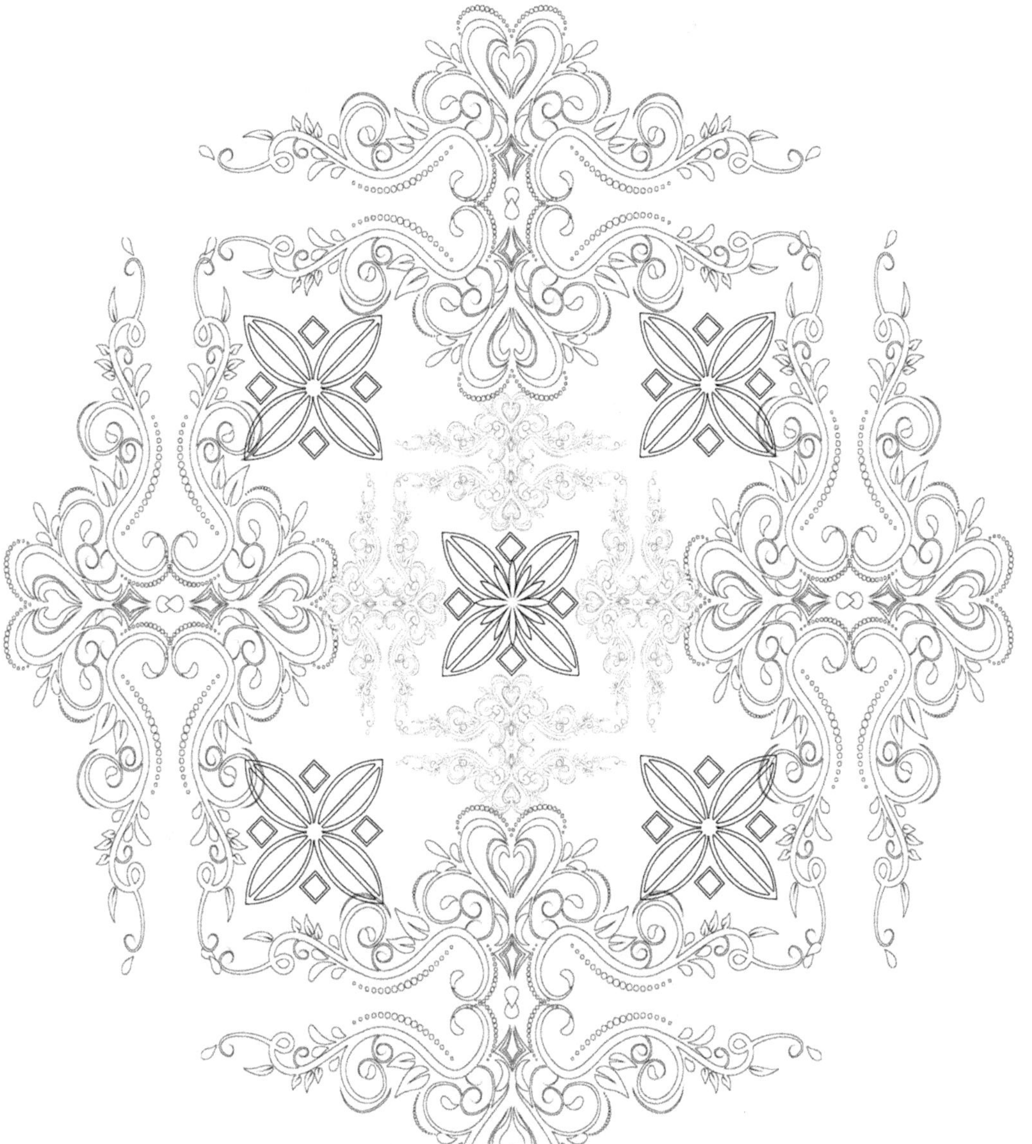

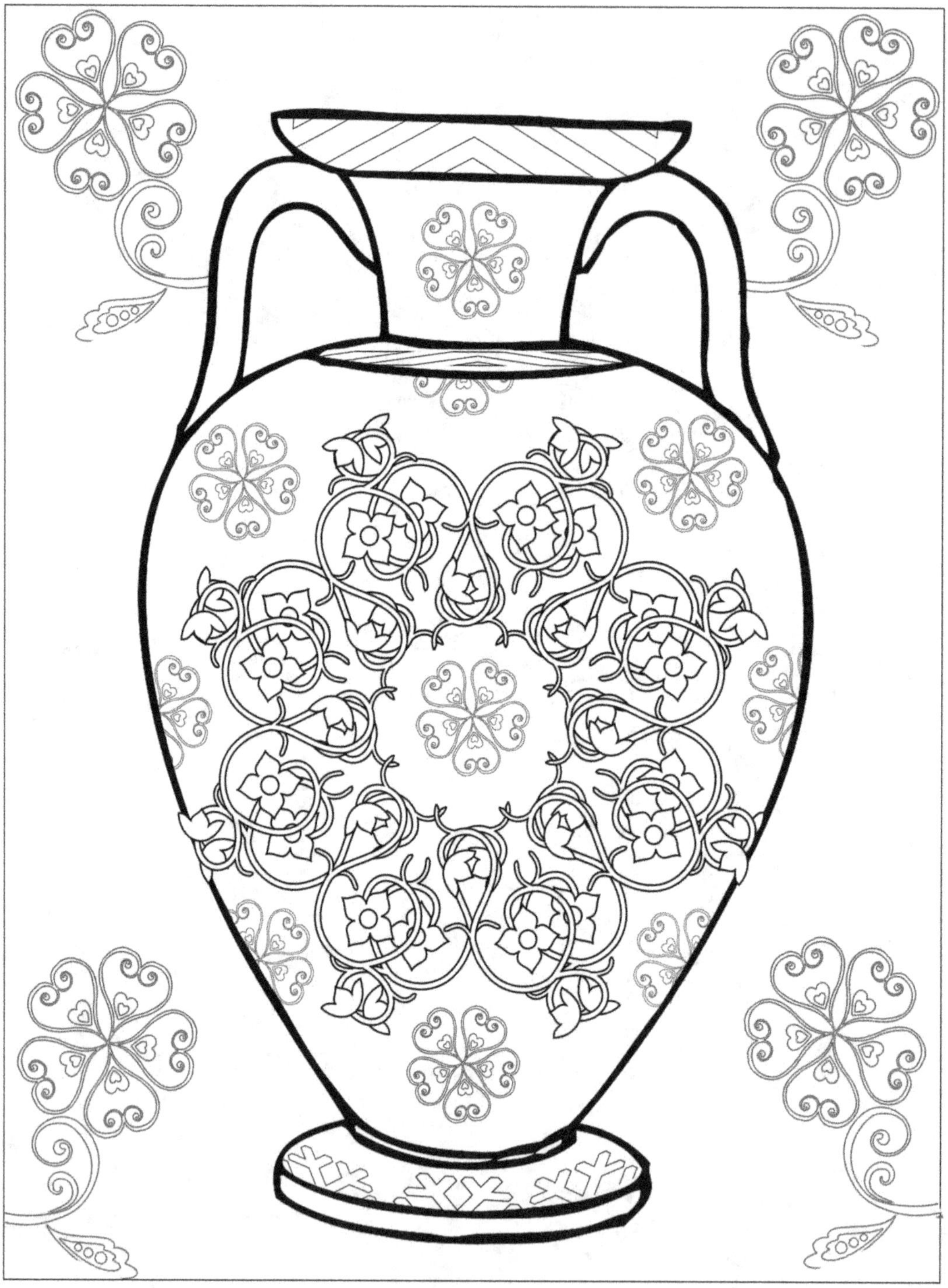

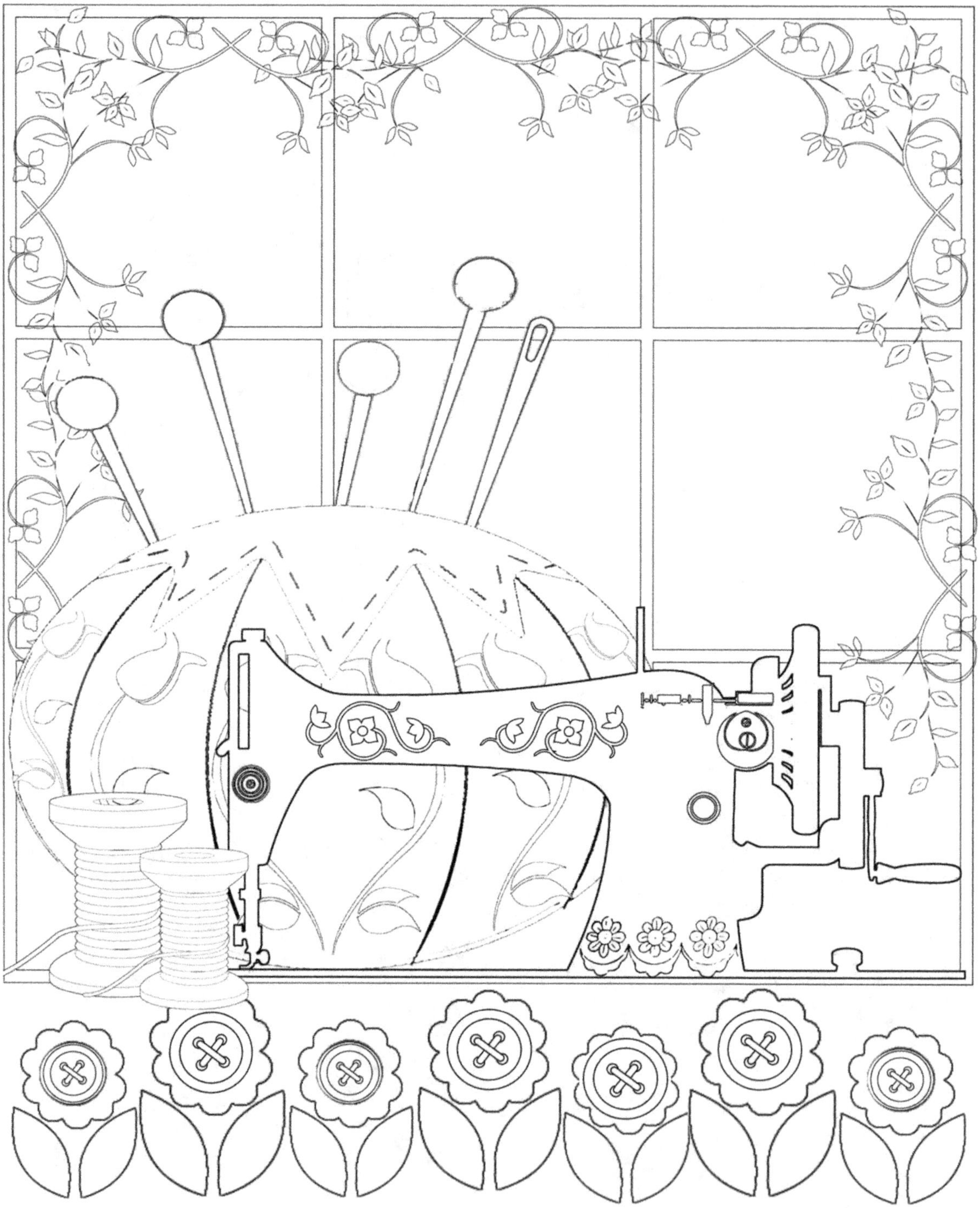

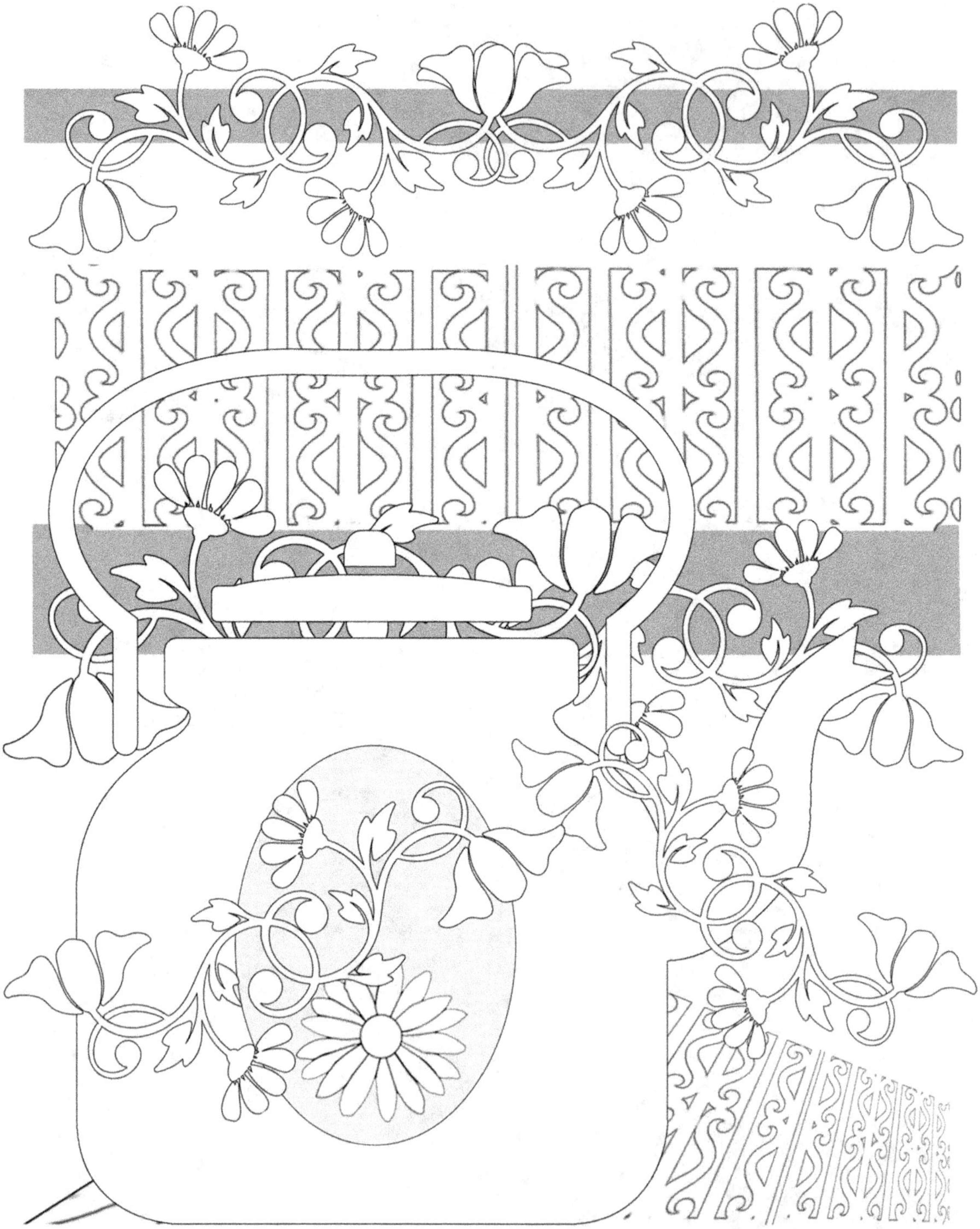

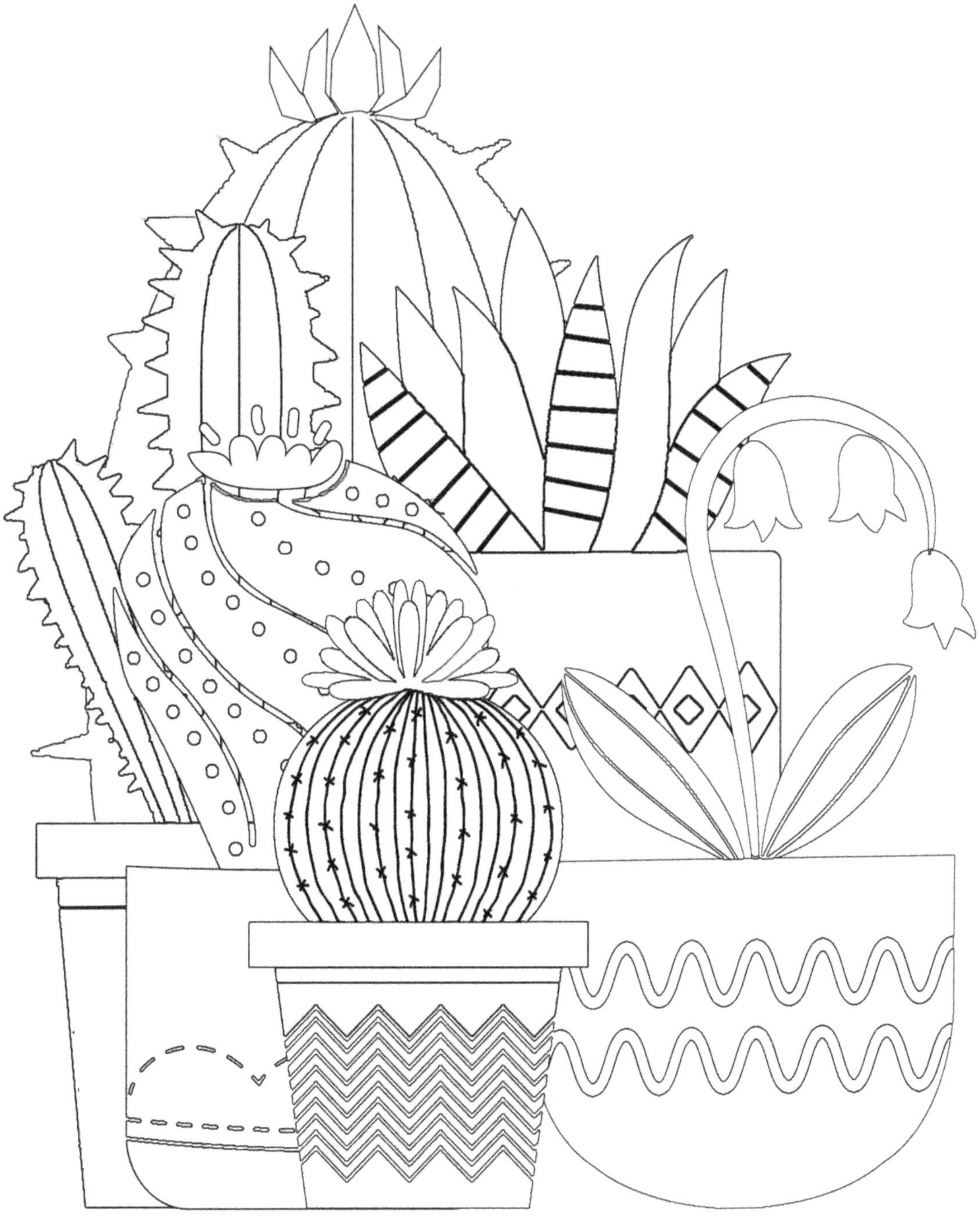

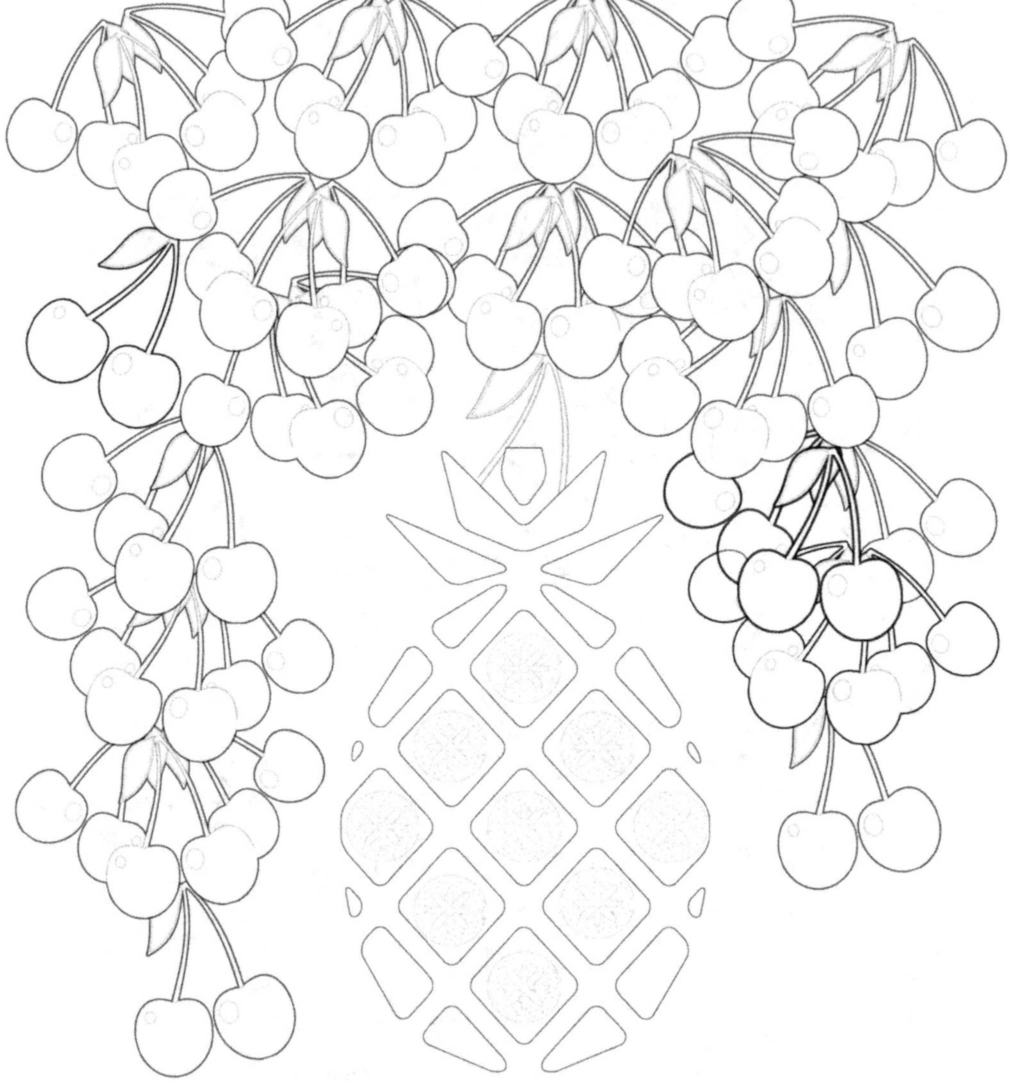

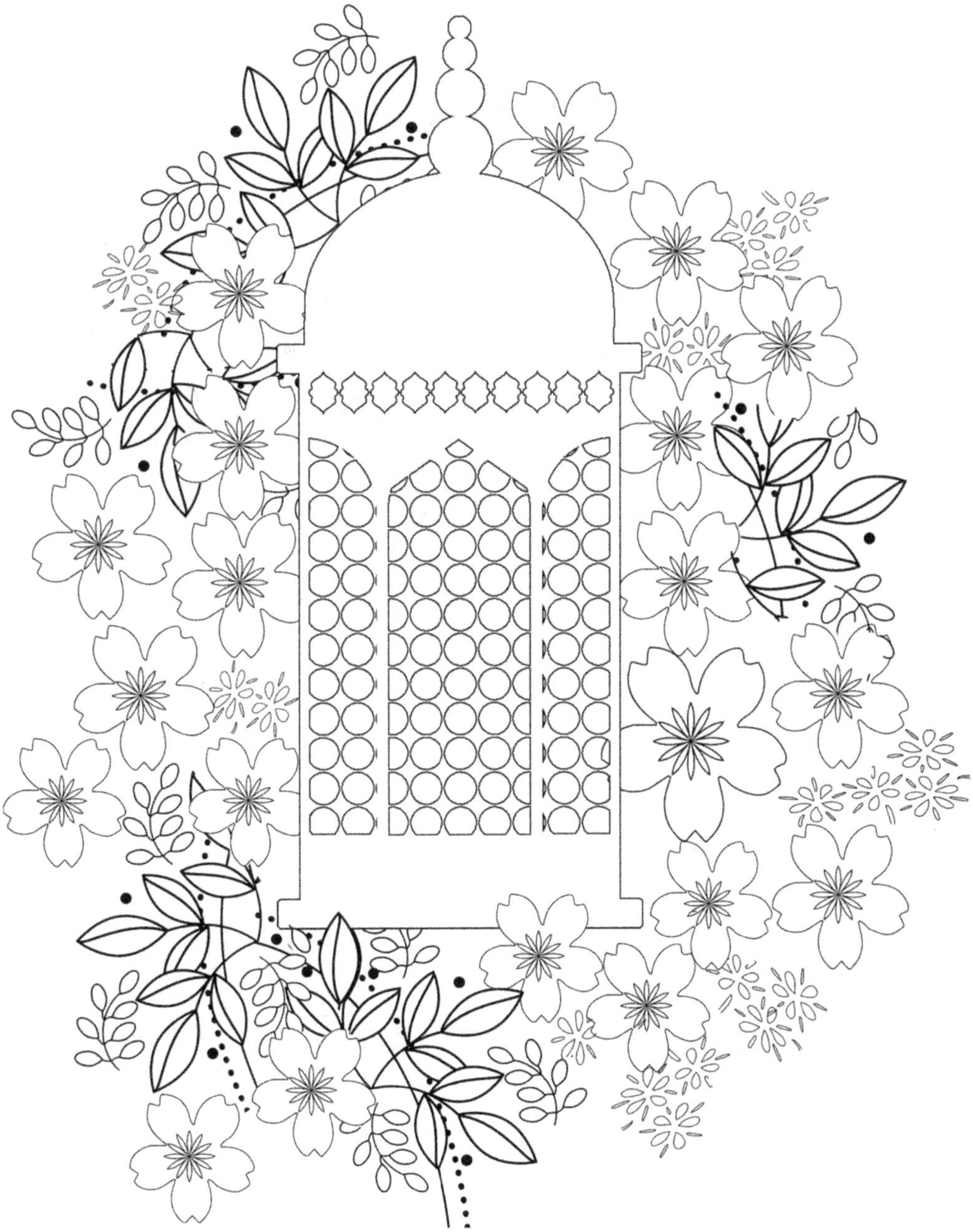

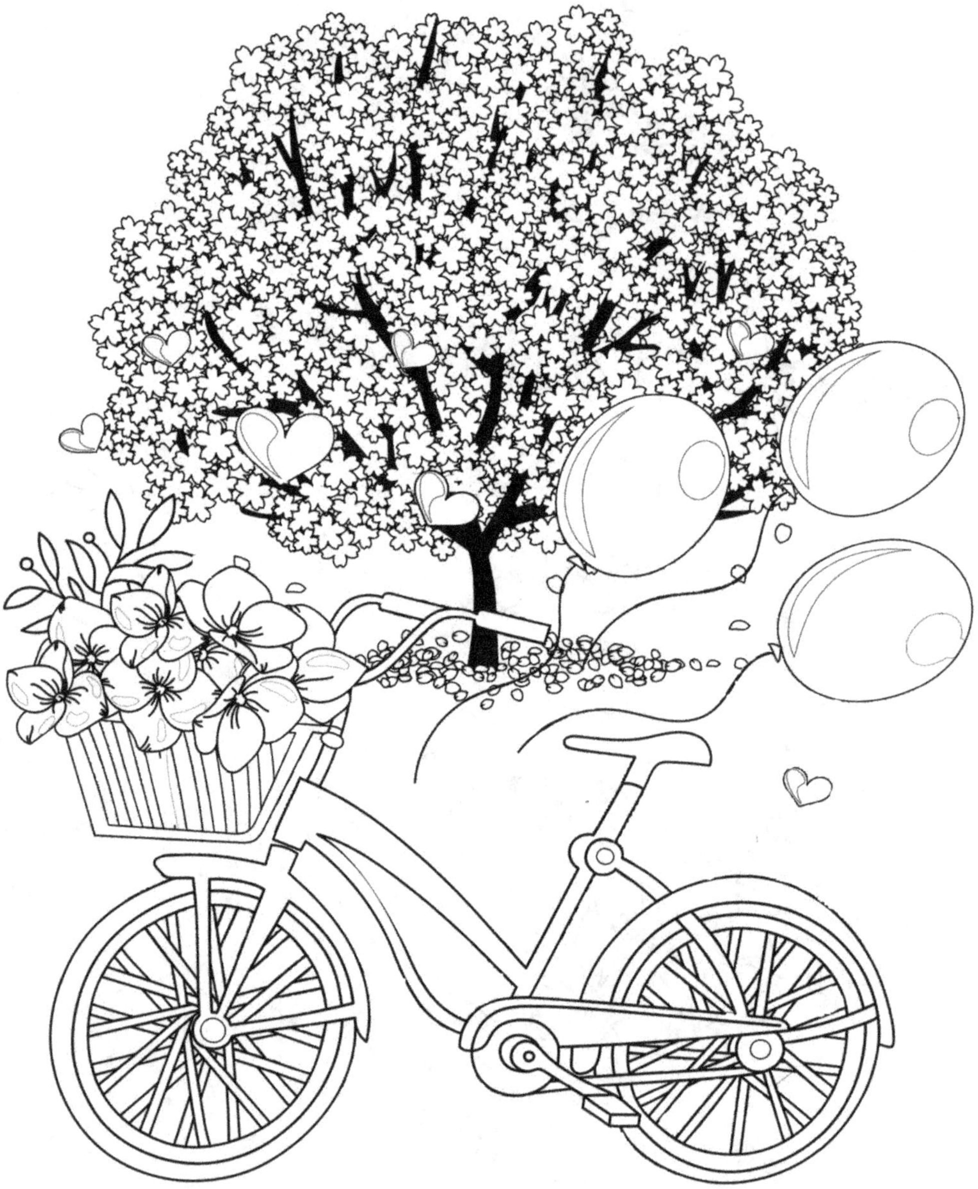

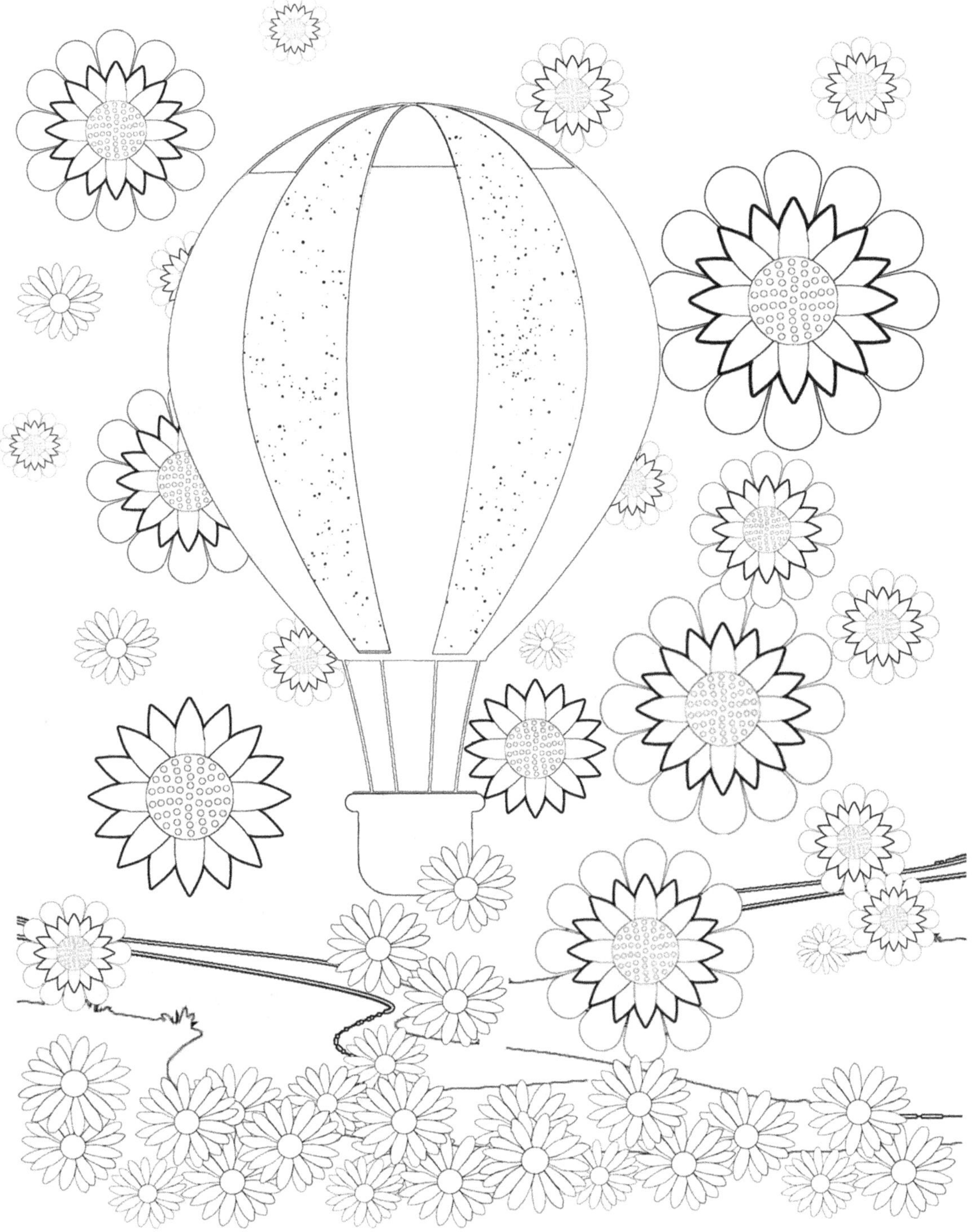

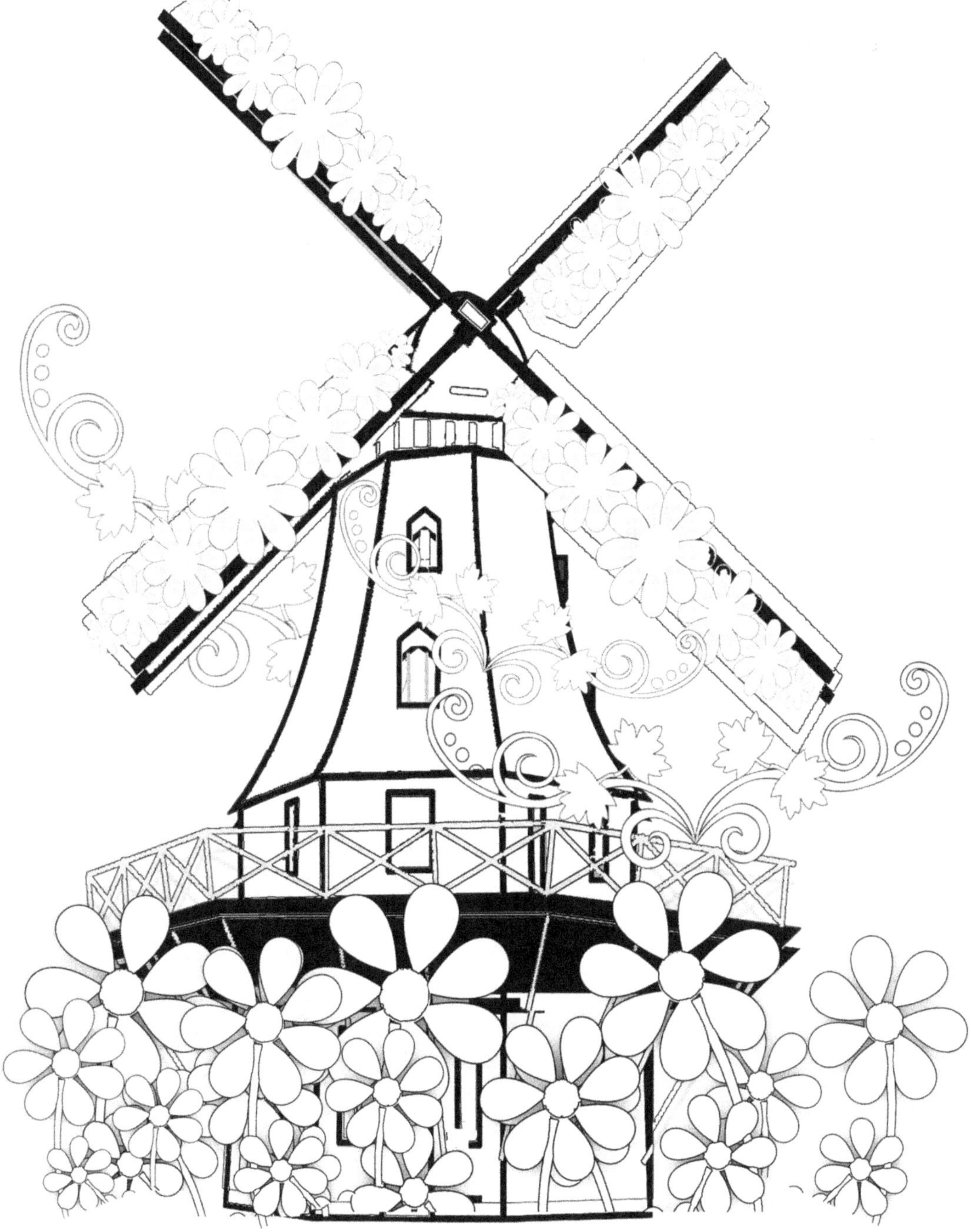

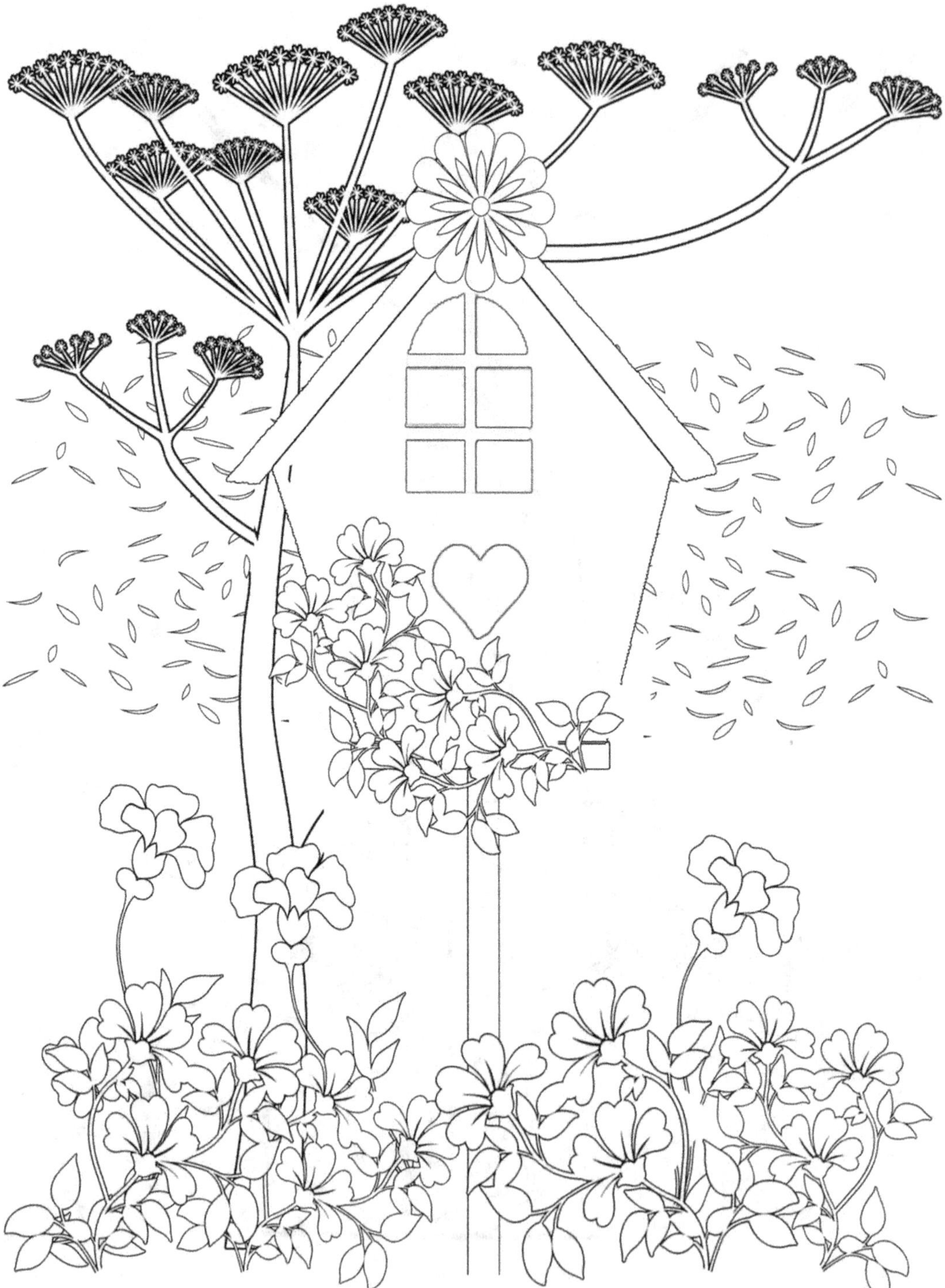

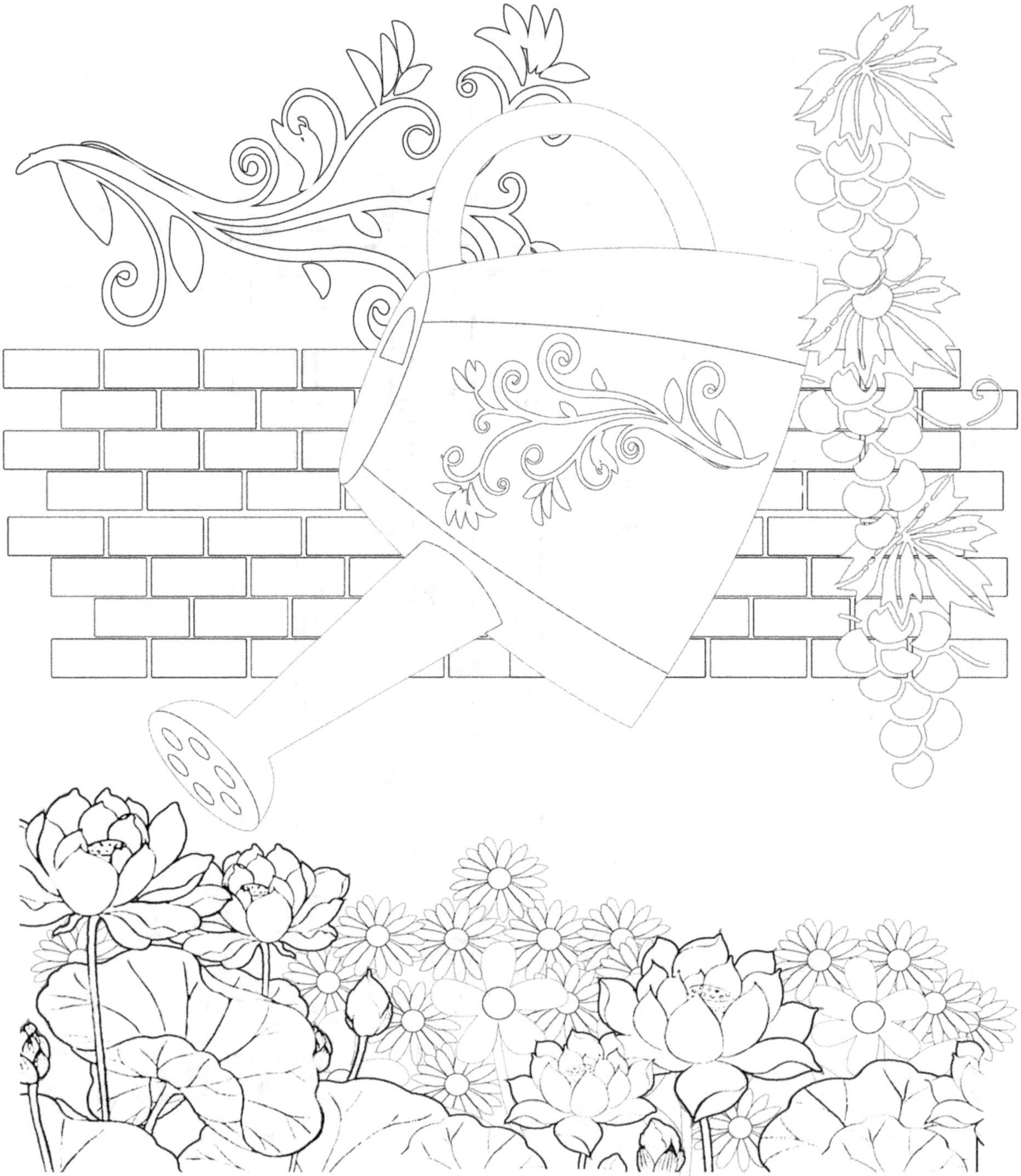

this book

belongs to :

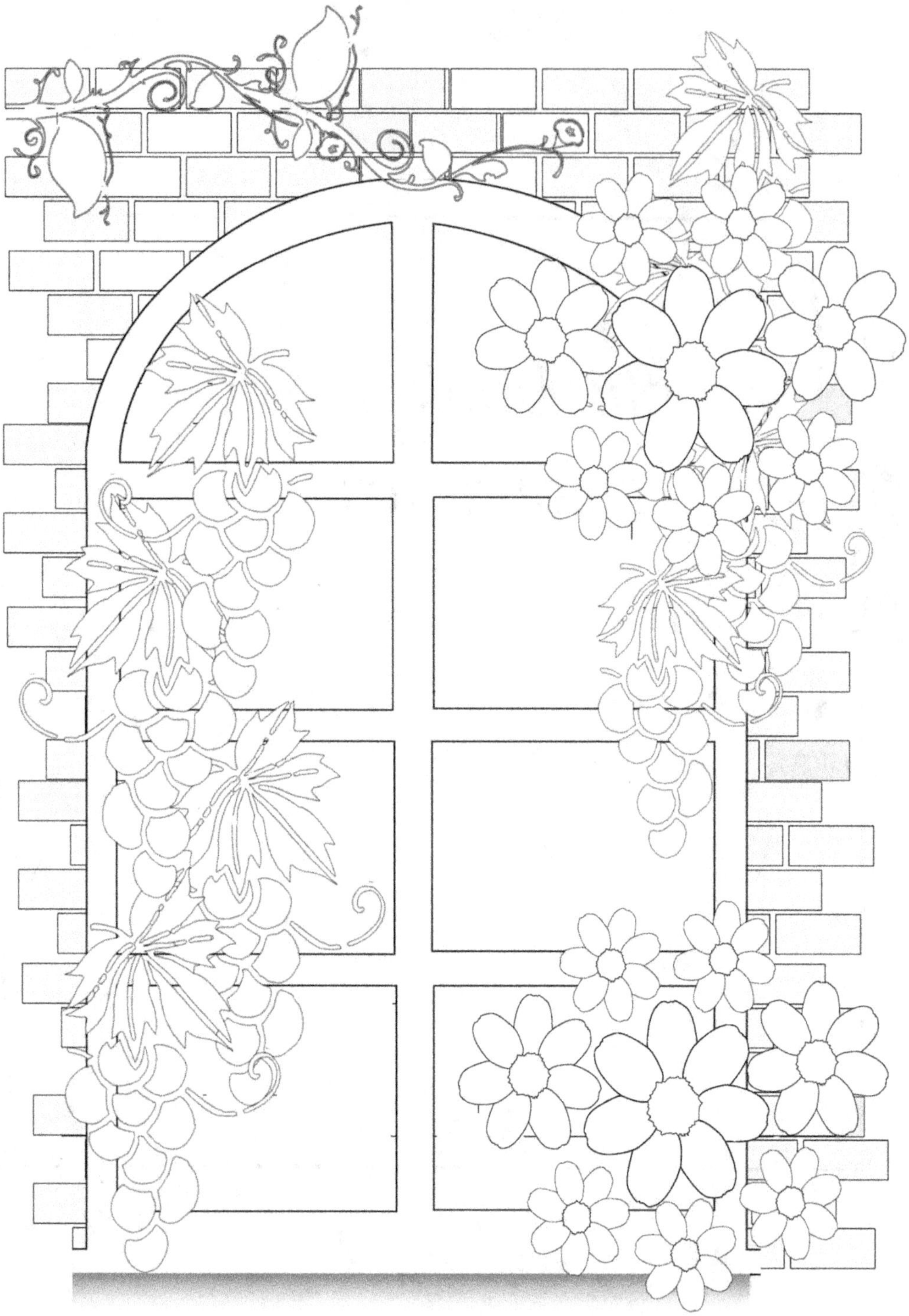

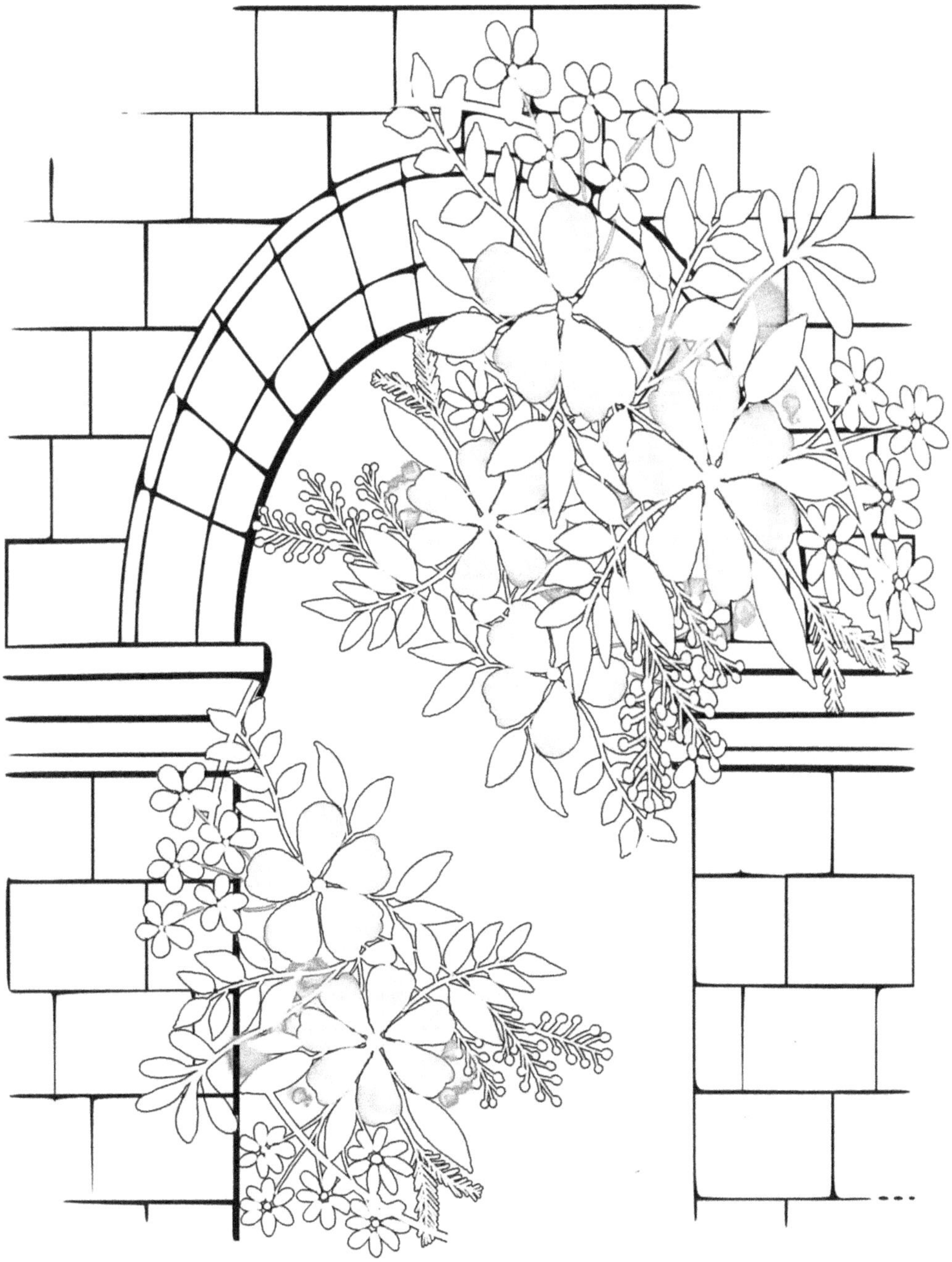

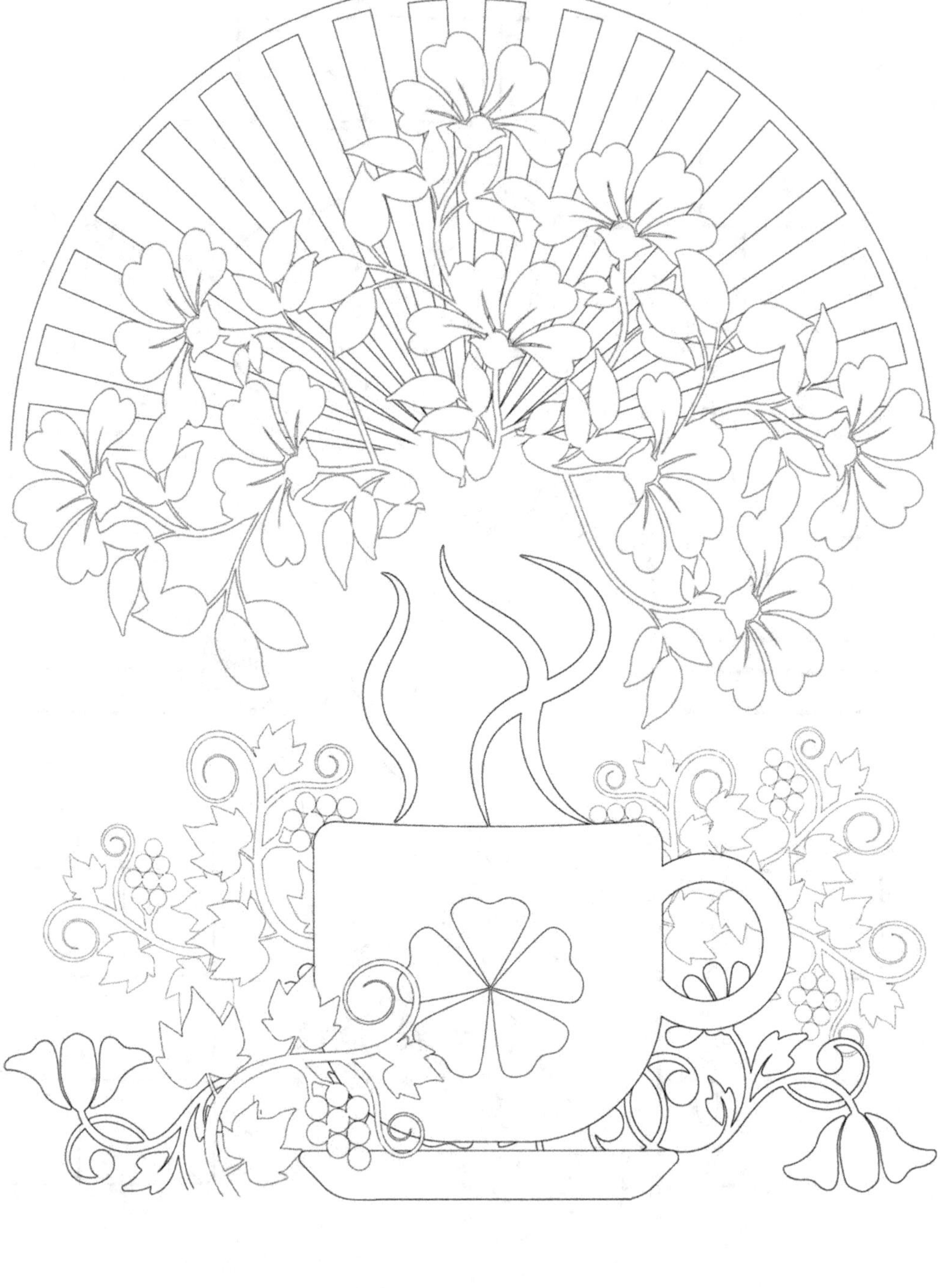

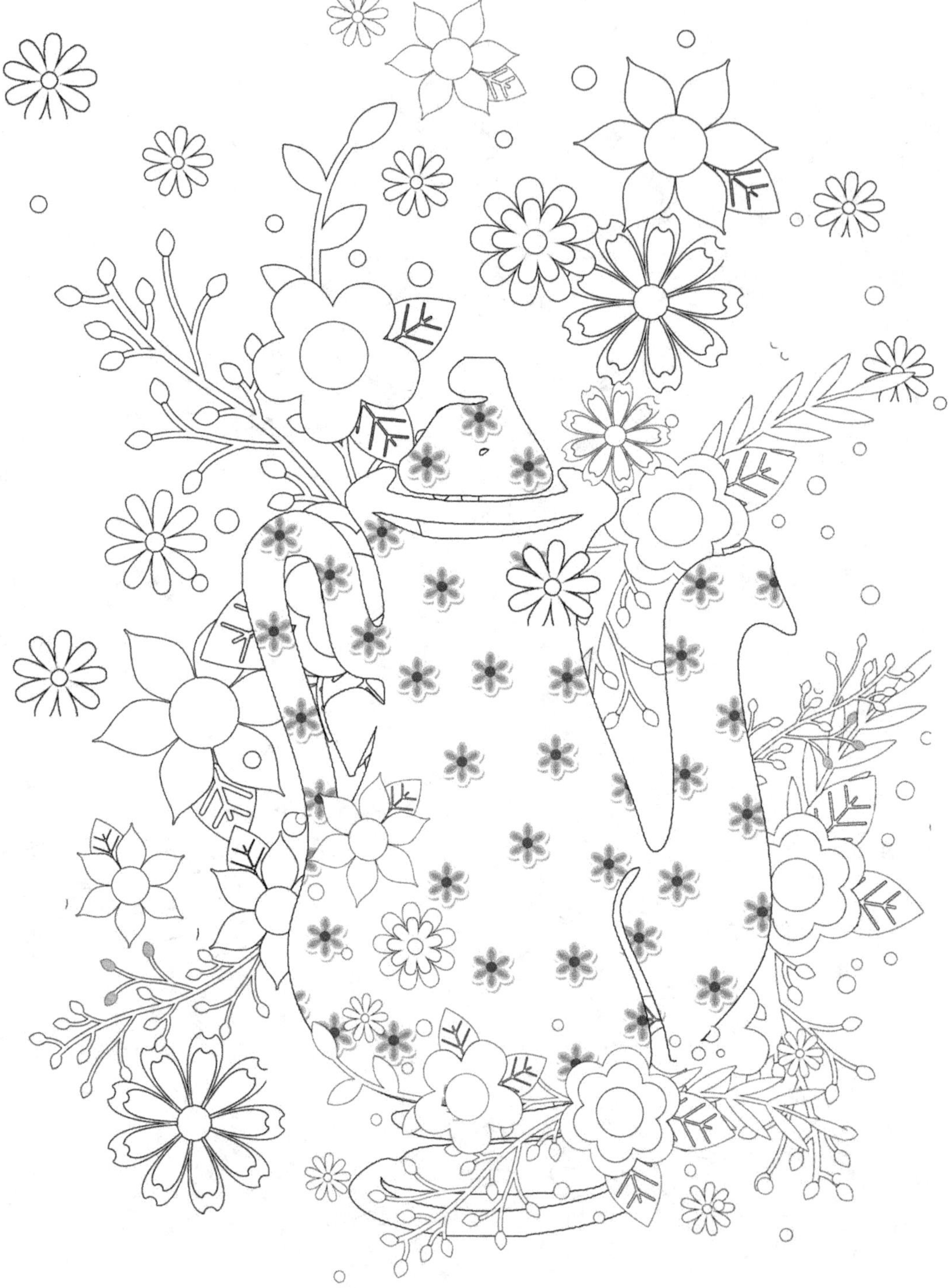

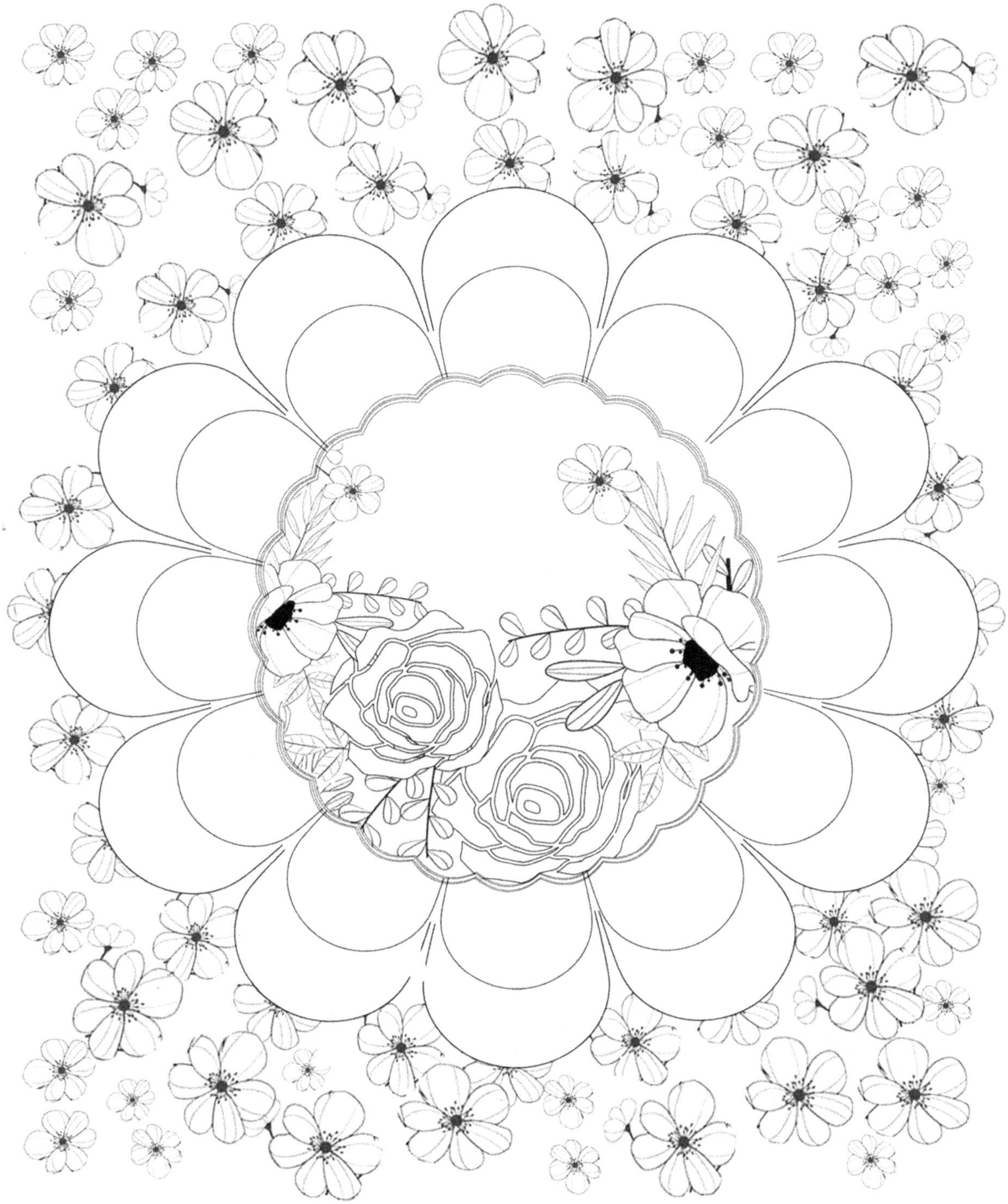

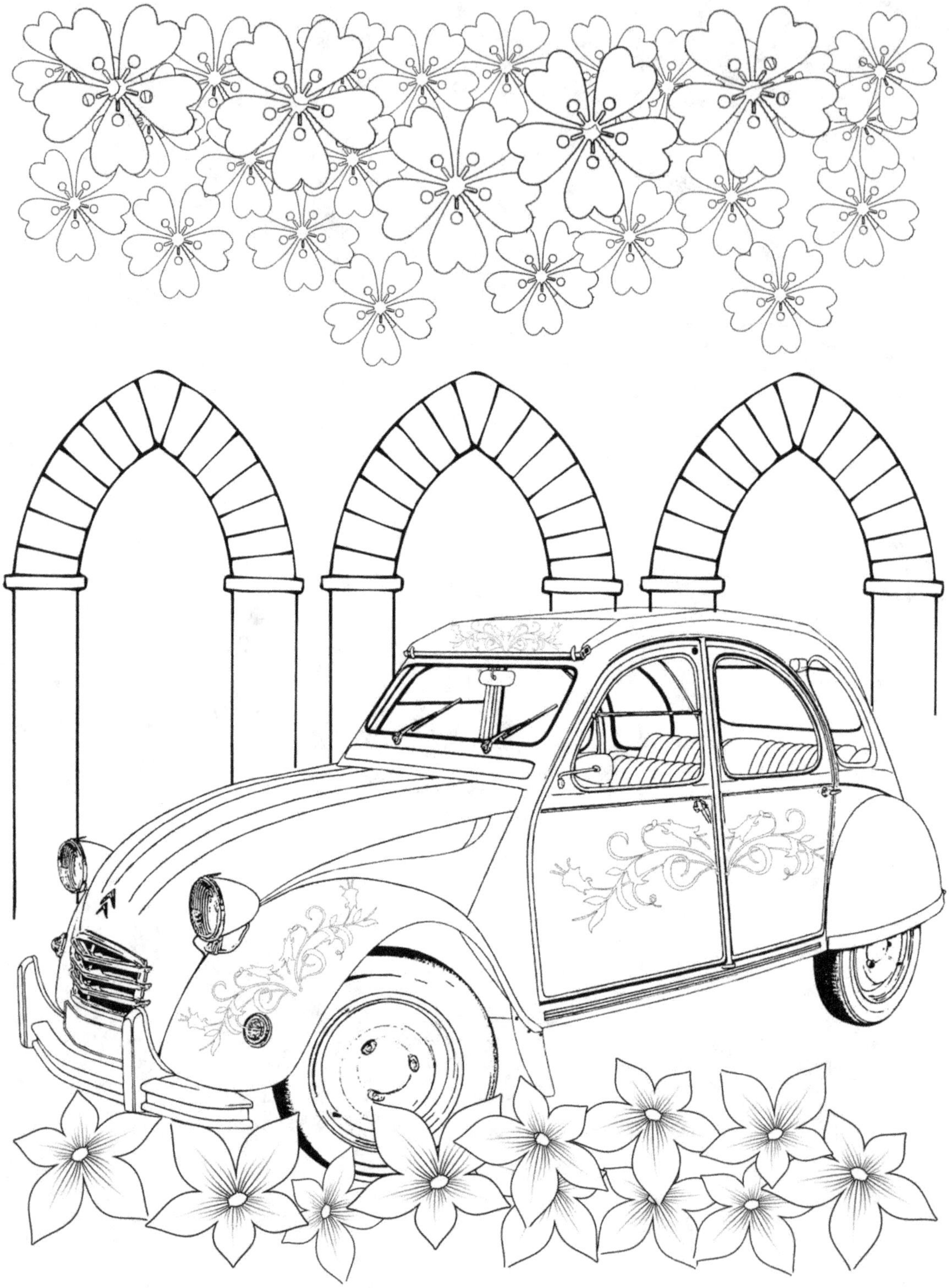

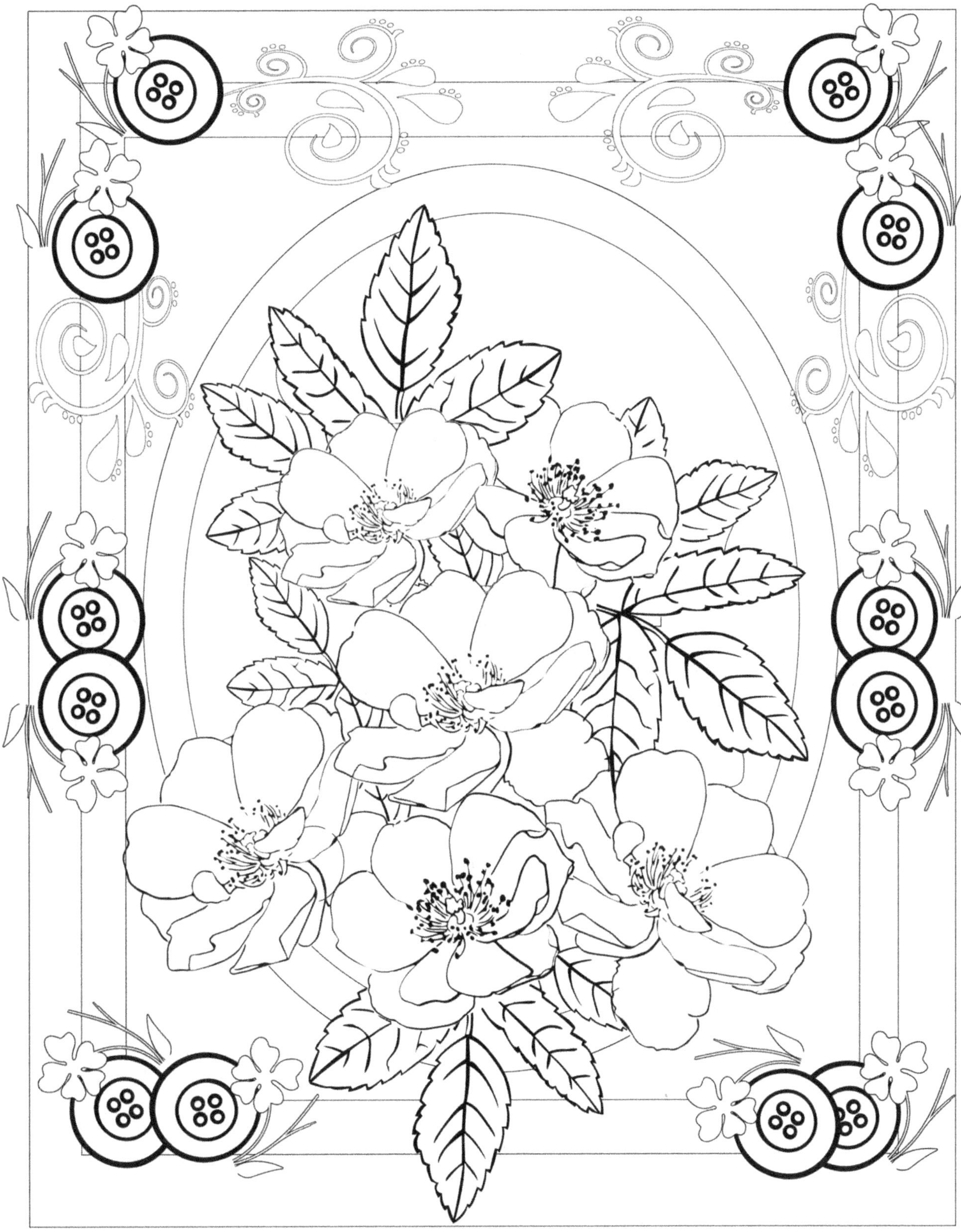

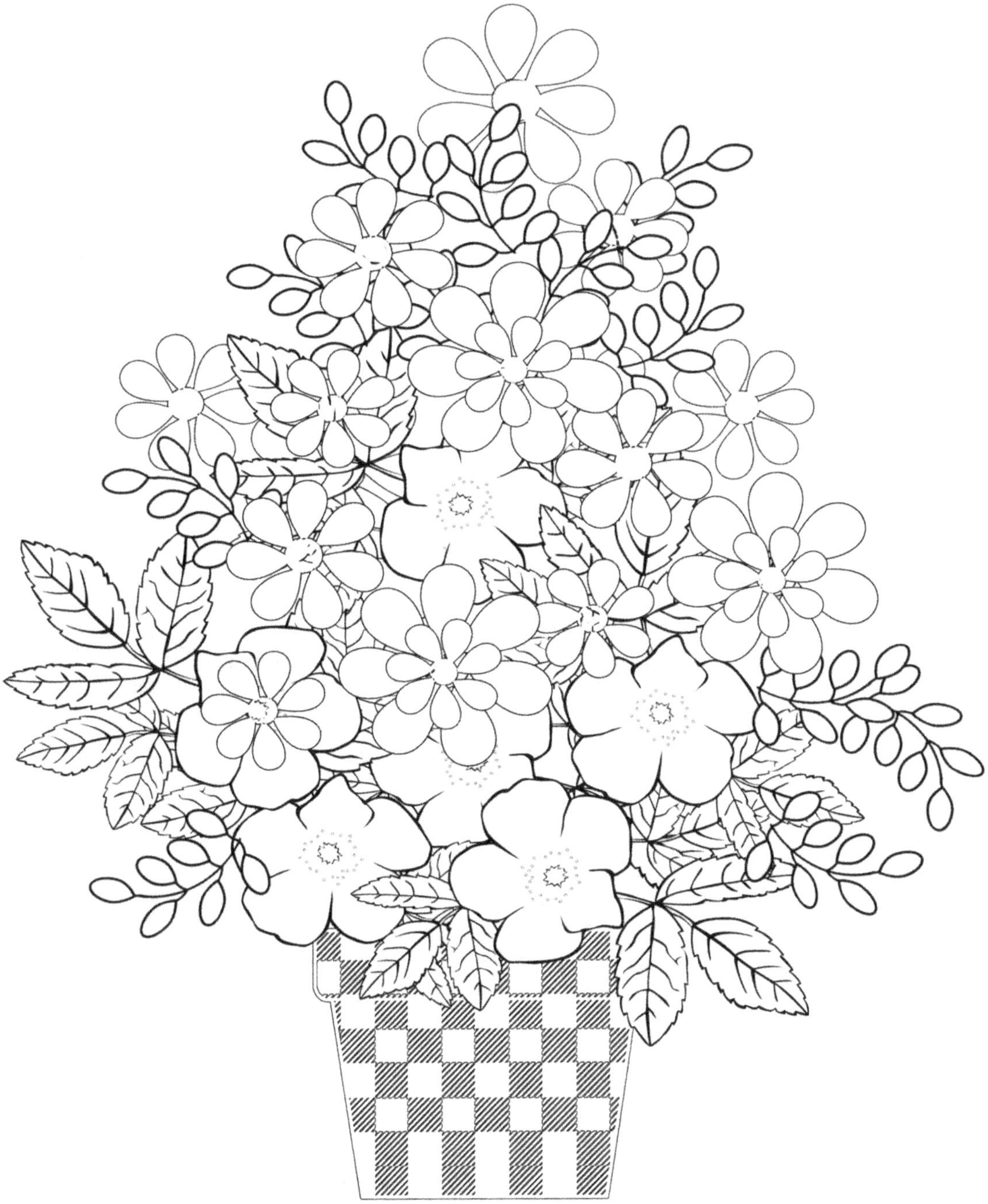

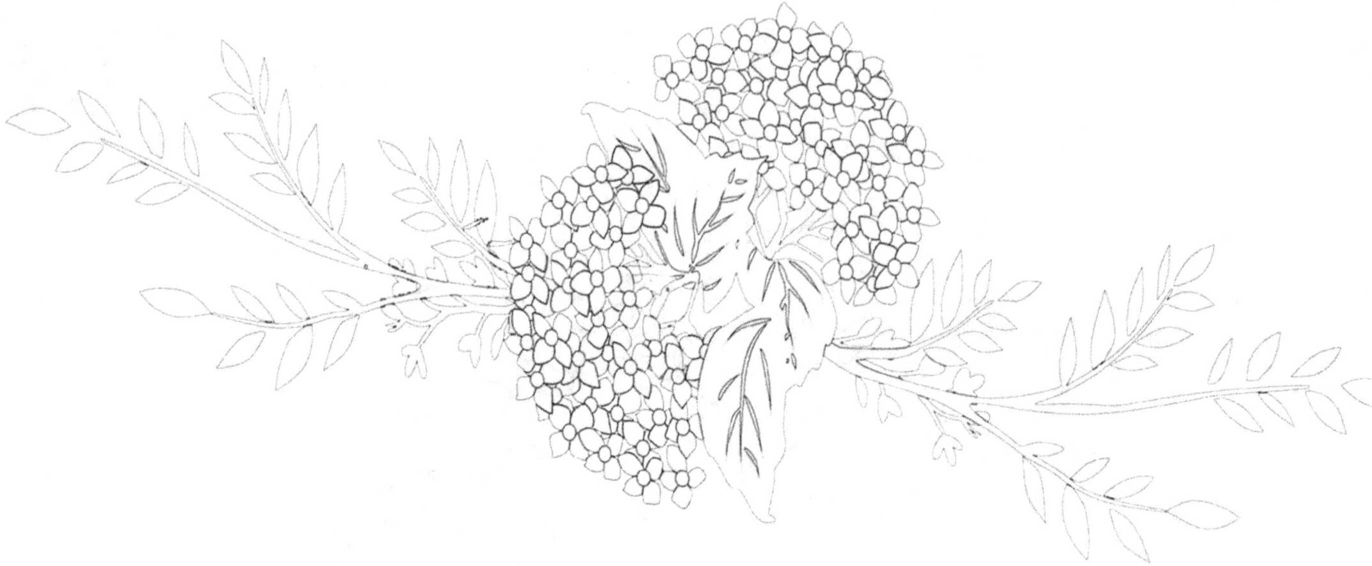

flowers coloring book

by layla l. rose

www.ingramcontent.com/pod-product-compliance
Lightning Source LLC
Chambersburg PA
CBHW081704220526
45466CB00009B/2882
* 9 7 8 1 6 5 8 7 4 3 5 9 4 *